Mutti
and
Papa

A LOVE STORY

Bill Franz

BILL FRANZ

 FriesenPress

Suite 300 - 990 Fort St
Victoria, BC, V8V 3K2
Canada

www.friesenpress.com

Thank you to Jon Isaak, Director, Centre for Mennonite Brethren Studies (CMBS)
in Winnipeg for permission to cite references to Halbstadt and the use of maps from
Helmut T. Huebert's Molotschna Historical Atlas. Thank you to Conrad Stoesz, Archivist,
Mennonite Heritage Archives in Winnipeg for scanning maps and for permission to use
downloaded maps from William Schroeder and Helmut T. Huebert in the Molotschna
Historical Atlas.

ISBN
978-1-03-910700-7 (Hardcover)
978-1-03-910699-4 (Paperback)
978-1-03-910701-4 (eBook)

1. BIOGRAPHY & AUTOBIOGRAPHY, HISTORICAL

Distributed to the trade by The Ingram Book Company

DEDICATION

This biography is dedicated to Mutti and Papa, my parents, in appreciation of their love for each other and their dedication to their family, their faith, and their community. They grew up in difficult circumstances during the late 1920s and '30s and into the second World War.

This book is also dedicated to our grandparents, to the opas (grandfathers) and oma (grandmother) we did not meet, to the oma we did grow up with and to the step-grandfather who raised Mutti as his own and was our opa. "Oma in Russland" was deported to Siberia and we knew her through cards, letters and photos. Finally, this book is dedicated to our children and grandchildren.

ACKNOWLEDGEMENTS

I would like to thank my family for their love, support, and encouragement with this project. It's been a work of many years in preparation. In particular, I would like to thank my sisters Margaret Wonko, Ingrid Pawlosky, and Monika Franz-Lien and my aunt Lydia Dyck and my uncle Hardy Rupp. In many ways this is their story too, especially for Aunt Lydia and Uncle Hardy who were born in German-occupied Poland during World War II and lived their childhoods in its aftermath. They came to Canada as young children and experienced first-hand the adjustments their family had to make in transitioning from the reality of war to starting over in a new land. Their parents, our Opa and Oma Rupp (Johann Jakob and Amalie) were then in their mid-forties with two young children, faced with having to learn a new language, find work, and establish a new home. In some respects it would have been easier for my parents, Johann and Ella, who were in their early twenties, to adjust. All of them, though, had lived through ten years of turmoil.

Lydia Dyck and Hardy Rupp shared their memories and stories heard. Monika Franz-Lien and Lydia Dyck helped with the editing and clarification of dates and later events. My daughter Anna Franz advised on image quality and restored photos. My good friend Alan Stewart provided valuable advice, reviewed drafts and suggested how the story could be told. All their assistance is so appreciated.

I would also like to thank Dr. Arnold Neufeldt-Fast of Tyndale University in Toronto, for his encouragement to all of us in telling these stories before they are lost. Thank you to Jon Isaak, Director, Centre for Mennonite Brethren Studies (CMBS) in Winnipeg for permission to cite references to Halbstadt and the use of maps from Helmut T. Huebert's Molotschna Historical Atlas. Thank you to Conrad Stoesz, Archivist, Mennonite Heritage Archives in Winnipeg for scanning maps and for permission to use downloaded maps from William Schroeder and Helmut T. Huebert in the Molotschna Historical Atlas.

Thank you to Brent Wiebe, a Director of the Mennonite Historical Society of Alberta for his generous support in creating contemporary maps pertinent to the personal journeys of family members during World War Two and post-war. Brent is also the overseer of Trails of the Past, a website exploring our Russian Mennonite heritage. Thank you to the staff at FriesenPress who provided professional publishing services and have been a pleasure to work with.

Finally, I would like to thank my dear wife Pearl Franz. Her support has been invaluable.

Contents

I.

Introduction

I was born in Canada in the mid-1950s to immigrant parents that had met as young people in a refugee camp in West Germany. Mutti and Papa (Mom and Dad) had been born in what is now Ukraine, but in different countries at the time. Borders kept shifting as a result of war. My first language was German and in many respects my childhood was similar to other children born to immigrant parents in our community.

We lived in a working-class neighbourhood, Winnipeg's West End (also known as Winnipeg Centre). My grandparents and aunt and uncle lived on the next street over, just a couple of blocks away. We attended First Mennonite Church in our neighbourhood where there were many families just like ours, with three or four kids.

I grew up knowing that I had family in Russia, my paternal grandmother "Oma in Russland" who lived in Siberia with her daughter and son-in-law and their children. I knew my paternal grandfather had disappeared during the war, my father had been wounded several weeks before the war ended while serving in the German Army (the Wehrmacht), and that he could not go back to see his mother and sister.

What to make of Papa's war service in the Wehrmacht of Nazi Germany? As his son, I've been reflecting on this for more than fifty years.

In Grade Five I was selected to recite John McCrae's war poem "In Flanders Fields" at the elementary school's Remembrance Day Service. John McCrae was a Canadian soldier, physician, and poet in the First World War. He wrote this poem in 1915, the day after one of his closest friends was killed in the fighting

1

and buried in a makeshift grave with a simple wooden cross. Every school child in Canada learns this poem, which begins with "In Flanders fields the poppies blow, between the crosses, row on row...". The red poppies that McCrae refers to are still worn in Canada and other countries of the British Commonwealth in the days leading up to Remembrance Day.

My father had the day off from work that Remembrance Day and I remember him raking leaves in the yard. I asked him, "Papa, what do you think of on Remembrance Day?" He answered, "I think of all the people who died."

As a young teenager in Grade Eight or so, I challenged my father with the words "Did you ever kill anyone?" His face turned red, he answered "No", and he walked away. A couple of years later I asked Mr. Karl Fast, a German teacher I respected, "What is war like?" His face turned red. He said, "War is hell" and turned away. I've never forgotten Mr. Fast's reaction. It informs my thoughts on war to this day.

I was raised in the Mennonite tradition, which historically includes pacifism as church doctrine. The peace position of the church interprets "You shall not kill" (one of the Ten Commandments) as literal and applies to armed conflict between nations. Hence Mennonites have traditionally refused military service and sought instead to perform alternate service as Conscientious Objectors.

Yet my father volunteered to join the Wehrmacht. It was important to him that we understood that. I can understand that for a sixteen-year old boy whose father and uncles had been taken away into forced labour by the Soviets, a fate he narrowly avoided, the Wehrmacht would have been seen as liberators. News of the outside world was tightly controlled in Stalin's regime and it is likely that most inhabitants of the Mennonite towns and villages in the Molotschna colony would not have heard much, if anything, about the oppression of the Jewish people by the Nazis.

My father said that he was glad that he had volunteered for the Wehrmacht in 1941, as the boys who had not were drafted in 1943 and they were drafted into the SS. He said "it would have been worse". A classmate of his who sat on the same bench was drafted into the SS and was sent in to quell the Warsaw Ghetto Uprising (and perished in that action). My father did say, "It was terrible what happened to the Jews".

Probably the best answer I can give in reflection on his war service is his reflection "those were not normal times". I can't argue that my father was not complicit as he served in the Wehrmacht, the armed forces of Nazi Germany. Although I understand from his account that he did not kill anyone personally, certainly his role as a translator and field messenger enabled the war effort.

After his death, one of my sisters went to the German Consulate in Winnipeg to advise of his passing. He was receiving a small pension from the German government for his military service. The woman at the Consulate said, much to the surprise of my sister, "He was in the SS. They all were." This disturbed my sisters and I greatly.

When I inquired of the Deutsche Dienststelle of his military record, I received the results with some trepidation. What did he really do in the war? Did he tell the truth? What if he hadn't told us everything? However, to my relief, the limited records corroborated what he had told us. I cannot think of any situation in which our father lied to us. I do believe him.

German guilt is something that I've wrestled with for many years. Not the guilt perhaps of those who served on the other side of the conflict, but rather the guilt that you feel because your father and perhaps your grandfather served in the Wehrmacht or other forces of Nazi Germany. I asked a cousin of mine who grew up in the Soviet Union after the war what she thought. She said. *"Die das haben Schlechtes getan sind tot und sind verantwortlich"* (those who have committed evil are dead and will have to answer for it). I understand this to mean that there may not be justice in this world, but there will be judgement in the next. I understand that several faiths (e.g. Judaism, Christianity and Islam) teach that believers will have to give an account in the afterlife of their actions in this life.

Seventy-five years have passed since the end of World War II and yet the subject continues to loom large in both national and social discourse.

World War II was the deadliest military conflict in history.[1] Estimates of total dead (for both military and civilian deaths) vary widely from thirty-five million to sixty million.

There has been renewed interest in Mennonite circles in historical analysis and revisiting accounts of those "not normal times".

....

1   Hughes, Thomas A., John Graham Royde-Smith, and The Editors of Encyclopaedia Britannica, *Costs of the war*. https://www.britannica.com/event/World-War-II/Costs-of-the-war.

Aileen Friesen writes in "Soviet Mennonites, the Holocaust & Nazism: Part 1"[2], "Direct Mennonite participation in the Holocaust is a fact. Even before Gerhard Rempel published an article attesting to this point in the *Mennonite Quarterly Review*, the first chair in Mennonite Studies at the University of Winnipeg, Harry Loewen, who also was a Soviet Mennonite, published the following: "Some [Soviet] Mennonite young men joined the German forces voluntarily and gladly, or at least did not resist induction...Some Mennonites even took part in "actions" against Jews..."[3]

Our parents, Mutti and Papa, were caught up in the cataclysmic events of those "not normal times" as were many others. My father in particular was afraid of falling into Soviet hands and being executed or sent to Siberia. He and my mother had survived and, as young people, hoped to create a new life for themselves far from the blood-stained soil of Europe.

....

2   Aileen Friesen, "Soviet Mennonites, the Holocaust & Nazism: Part 1", *Anabaptist Historians*, April 25, 2017, https://anabaptisthistorians.org/author/afriesen77/.

3   Harry Loewen, "A Mennonite-Christian View of Suffering: The Case of Russian Mennonites in the 1930s and 1940s," *The Mennonite Quarterly Review* 77, no. 1 (January 2003): 55.

2.

The Ancestors of
Johann Franz

The Franzes were descended from Low German Mennonites who had left the Groningen area (Friesland) in what is now the north-east part of the Netherlands to escape religious persecution (possibly in 1540 or later during the sixteenth and seventeenth centuries) and settled in the Vistula region of West Prussia (now Poland). Papa said that our forefathers came from Groningen. Mennonites were part of the Anabaptist movement of the Radical Reformation of the 1500s and were persecuted for their beliefs in believer's baptism (adult baptism), a refusal to bear arms and a refusal to swear oaths of loyalty to the state.[4] "Migration Chronology of an Old Flemish Congregation in Polish-Prussia" by William Schroeder (see Map One) lists the following dates: "Groningen to Przechovka 1540, Przechovka to Brenkenhofswalde 1764, and Brenkenhofswalde to Gnadenfeld, Molotschna 1834". "Brenkenhofswalde, Franztal, and Neudessau were located along the Netze River between Driesen and Netzebruch". Prussia had offered refuge to the Mennonite farmers and craftsmen in exchange for their useful skills in draining land for agriculture, but Mennonites were subsequently forbidden to enlarge their landholdings by Friedrich Wilhelm II of Prussia in 1787. Further restrictions were implemented in 1789 and 1801 with the aim of undermining the Mennonite principle of nonresistance. Prussia was becoming increasingly militaristic. The land in New

....

4   Wikipedia, s.v. "Mennonites," last modified on February 26, 2021, at 11:59 (UTC), https://en.wikipedia.org/wiki/Mennonites.

Russia (South Russia) that Catherine the Great's armies had conquered from the Turks and her invitation to German settlers began to look more inviting.[5]

Meanwhile, a family by the name of Unruh, migrated in 1834 from the Brenkenhofswalde, Brandenburg/Neumark area of West Prussia and settled in the Molotschna area. At the age of fifty-three, Martin Unruh, along with his wife Sara (née Voth), then forty years old, and their seven children ranging in age from two to sixteen received permission to emigrate on February 2,1833 from Brenkenhofswalde/Friedeberg to Russia.[6] The colonists travelled overland to Chortitza (the "Old Colony" founded in 1789 on the Dnieper River), over-wintered there, and then travelled on to the Molotschna in 1834. They settled in Gnadenfeld, which was founded in 1835. Martin Unruh would have been born in about 1780 and Sara in about 1793. Maria Unruh, eleven years at the time, having been born in about 1822, was the third child of Martin and Sara. It was she who would grow up to marry Heinrich Franz (who had also emigrated from Prussia) and were Johann's great-grandparents. Maria died in 1872 and Heinrich followed in 1880 in nearby Sparrau. Maria and Heinrich had nine children, of which David was the sixth. David Franz married Katherina Fast and were grandparents of Johann (Katherina died in 1937 in Nieder Chortitza).

Pioneering conditions are usually difficult, particularly when land is broken to the plough. Colonists can struggle to establish themselves. Here is an extract from "My Life Story" by Anna Braun, a daughter of Heinrich and Maria Franz and a younger sister to David:

> *"I, Anna Braun, will attempt to record my life story, as well as I can remember it.*
>
> *I was born April 12, 1868 in South Russia, in the village of Gnadenfeld, juris-dictions of Taurien and Berdjansk. My father was Henry Franz; mother was née Maria Unruh. Both emigrated as young people from Prussia to Russia, where they became engaged to be married. They belonged to the Mennonite*

5   Krahn, Cornelius, *Molotschna Mennonite Settlement (Zaporizhia Oblast, Ukraine)*, Global Anabaptist Mennonite Encyclopedia Online, 1957, last modified on February 13, 2021, at 15:48, https://gameo.org/index.php?title=Molotschna_Mennonite_Settlement_(Zaporizhia_Oblast,_Ukraine)&oldid=167714.

6   Thiessen, Richard D., *Migration of Mennonites from Brandenburg, Prussia to Russia 1833-35*, accessed February 26, 2021, http://www.mennonitegenealogy.com/russia/brandenburgmennonite-combined.htm.

Church of Gnadenfeld. Here they settled as well. They had a small farm of 15 dessiatines (40.5 acres or 16.4 hectares). They had a family of ten children, of which one died in childbirth. Nine became adults, of which I was the youngest. When I was four, my mother died. The oldest two brothers were married by then, but still lived in the family dwelling. The oldest was a carpenter, and the second a blacksmith. They were both self-employed, whereas three other brothers and a sister had to find jobs. I and the oldest sister and the youngest brother stayed with father. Our parents were always poor. Mother was often sickly. Often they suffered from crop failures, cattle diseases, and too little land. As a result of a series of misfortunes they got into debt. And when mother died, the creditors came and wanted their money. Because father was unable to pay, everything was recorded. The local authorities came with a number of men and wrote everything down. Father was also a cabinet maker. So we had quality furniture, but everything was written down, including horses and wagons; only one cow we were allowed to keep. House and acreage - everything became the target of creditors; only the workbench, a bed for father and a bunk for me and my sister who was nearly blind (otherwise she would have to find a job also).

I began school at this time. I didn't get far in school. Because I too suffered from poor eyesight, I missed school frequently.

When I was twelve, we moved to Elizabethtal, where my oldest brother had rented a farm. So we joined them. Father went working out a lot after this. At house construction, he was a master carpenter. When he was fifty he had the misfortune to fall off the scaffolding of a shed they were building. He suffered internal injuries and lived only five days and died of a violent hemorrhage. We live in the hope that we will see our parents again in heaven. Mother was converted, and father lived a quiet lonely life. He did not go to church and the Mennonite Brethren church was not represented where they lived. But he was a man of prayer and was often absorbed with the Bible and hymnal."[7]

Johann's ancestors on his mother's side were the Nürnbergs, descended from German Lutheran colonists that had migrated to New Russia (or South Russia) in

....
7   Braun, Anna, *My Life* Story, unpublished account, April 1952.

1804 from the Württemberg area of south-west Germany (near Stuttgart).[8] South-west Germany was impacted greatly by the Napoleonic wars and many Germans (Roman Catholics, Lutherans, and Mennonites) emigrated to the Black Sea area.[9]

The Nürnbergs settled in Hoffental which was founded in 1804. Hoffental was located across the Molotschna (or Molochnaya) River from Halbstadt and just south of Prischib, the administrative centre of both Protestant (Lutheran) and Roman Catholic villages on the west side of the Molochnaya River (Prischib was also established in 1804). The Nürnbergs may have migrated to West Prussia (Poland) first in 1802. They may have floated directly down the Danube River in a Zille (Ulm box) to the Black Sea, or they may have migrated overland in a wagon train. Johann's great-great-grandparents were Wilhelm and Anna Nürnberg, Wilhelm having emigrated from Württemberg. Johann's great-grandfather Wilhelm Nürnberg, was born in 1827 in Hoffental. Johann's grandparents were Eduard Nürnberg, born July 20, 1868 in Andreburg (deceased in 1908) and Pauline (née Hilz), born in 1872 in Karlowka/Dnepropetrovsk (deceased August 14, 1902).

Elisabet Nürnberg (R) with siblings Anna, Paula and Hans 1900.

David D. Franz/Elisabet Nürnberg engagement 1912.

8   Wikipedia, s.v. "History of Germans in Russia, Ukraine and the Soviet Union," last modified on January 30, 2021, at 02:26 (UTC), https://en.wikipedia.org/wiki/History_of_Germans_in_Russia,_Ukraine_and_the_Soviet_Union.

9   Wikipedia, s.v. "Black Sea Germans," last modified on February 18, 2021, at 07:58 (UTC), https://en.wikipedia.org/wiki/Black_Sea_Germans.

Peter, David D., and Nikolaus Franz (L to R), Imperial Russian Army WW1.

David D. (Davidovich) Franz, Johann's father was born February 13, 1889 on the Steinbach Estate in the southernmost part of the Molotschna colony. Elisabet Nürnberg, Johann's mother, was born May 10, 1894 in Kankrinowka/ Dnepropetrovsk. David and Elisabet married in 1912 and had six children together.

Johann David Franz was born on February 24, 1925 to David D. Franz and Elisabet (née Nürnberg), in Andreburg, USSR (Union of Soviet Socialist Republics) in what is now Ukraine. Andreburg was a Lutheran village near the Molotschna settlement of the Mennonites and lay about twenty-one km northwest from Halbstadt (currently Molochans'k) Today Andreburg is called Chornozemne and lies about thirty-three km northwest of Tokmak. Halbstadt was one of two administrative centres of the Molotschna settlement, the other being Gnadenfeld.

Johann (known as Hans) lived with his parents and older sisters Käthe and Anna on the estate of his late grandfather Eduard Nürnberg, with his uncle Hans Nürnberg and family. Johann was the fifth of six children to be born to David and Elisabet. The first two, Eduard and Irma, died as small children. Käthe, born in 1915, died at the age of twelve in Andreburg. Anna was born in 1916. In 1930 the family moved to Halbstadt as a result of collectivization[10], the Soviet policy of seizing private land holdings without compensation for the purposes of state-run collective farms.[11] After their move to Halbstadt, their last child, Margaret (Gretel) was born on January 20, 1932. The family also lived in Tiegenhagen for a couple of years.

10   Froese, Peter F., *Collectivization in the Soviet Union,* Global Anabaptist Mennonite Encyclopedia Online, 1953, last modified on August 20, 2013, at 19:08, https://gameo.org/index. php?title=Collectivization_in_the_Soviet_Union&oldid=79788.

11   Wikipedia, s.v. "Collectivization in the Soviet Union," last modified on February 20, 2021, at 23:28 (UTC), https://en.wikipedia.org/wiki/Collectivization_in_the_Soviet_Union.

3.

The Ancestors of Ella Weber

The Webers originated in the Württemberg/Baden/Pfalz area of south-west Germany. As part of the Josephine colonization, the villages of Stanin and Hanunin were founded in 1797 by German Lutheran settlers. The Josephine colonization was a settlement campaign of the Austrian Empire to colonize new crown land wrested from the Ottoman Empire, in particular Galicia.[12] Wilhelm Friedrich Weber, who would become Ella's father, was born on May 13, 1888 in Hanunin, Galicia (between what is now known as Stanyn[13] and Radekhiv, Ukraine). This is all that is known about his origins.

Ella's maternal ancestors, the Schreyer family, originated in the Rhineland-Palatinate, a region in southwest Germany that includes the city of Trier (founded by the Romans) in the Moselle Valley. Seven generations of her family had lived in Dornfeld, a village founded in 1785 by German Lutherans as part of the Josephine colonization. Today the village is known as Ternopillya and is about 20 kilometres south of Lviv, formerly known as Lwów (Polish), Lemberg (German), and Lvov (Russian).

The village home on lot sixty-seven was last owned by her uncle Georg Schreyer and his wife Sofie Manz and previously by Ella's grandparents Georg Schreyer and his wife Katherine Rössler. The Rösslers had owned the home previous to the Schreyers for two generations before this, while the Schreyers

....

12   Wikipedia, s.v. "Kingdom of Galicia and Lodomeria," last modified on February 21, 2021, at 05:33 (UTC), https://en.wikipedia.org/wiki/Kingdom_of_Galicia_and_Lodomeria.

13   Wikipedia, s.v. "Stanyn," last modified February 12, 2021, at 11:39, https://de.wikipedia.org/wiki/Stanyn.

had owned the adjoining property on lot sixty-six for seven. In addition to the Schreyers, family names (maiden names) include Rössler, Lang, Manz, Harlfinger, Bechtloff, Maurer, Allenbacher, Schneeberger, Arnt, Hut, Kramer, Bartsherer, and Weinheimer.[14]

Amalie Katherine Adele Schreyer, who would become Ella's mother, had been born on December 18, 1907 in Dornfeld. In the beginning of World War I, Amalie's mother Katherine Schreyer (née Rössler) with her children, along with many other people of Dornfeld fled the fighting by horse and wagon to Pfaffstätten (near Vienna, Austria), a journey of about five hundred kilometres. Amalie (known as Mali) was seven years old. Her father Georg along with most of the men stayed behind. Georg rented an estate about seventy kilometres from Dornfeld which consisted of two properties three kilometres apart. He was no match for a group of men who came and stole all of their livestock, including thirty-six cows and two oxen. They only left two cows because the workers explained they were theirs. After a while Katherine and her children returned.

In the summer of 1916, a drunken Czech soldier who was in charge of some Russian prisoners of war, stabbed Mali's father Georg with a sword. One account says the soldier was upset about the quality of the water in the well and said it was undrinkable. Another account says the soldier was harassing a woman at the well and Georg intervened. Apparently the soldier was a friend of his and was overcome with remorse when he sobered up. The workers rushed over to the other property to bring Katherine and their children, eight-year-old Mali and three-year-old Mila (Emilie) in a horse-drawn carriage to see Georg as he lay dying. Upon seeing his family, he said to Katherine, "We will have to part. I will have to leave you and the children". He reached toward Mali and died.

As the war was still raging, Katherine and the children moved back to Dornfeld. Mali's maternal uncle, Leopold Rössler, had recently died from typhus in Zwornik, Bosnien (Zvornik, Bosnia). Katherine sold the Rössler family estates and received enough money that she could have purchased an apartment building in Lemberg. However the children's guardian, her father-in-law, wouldn't allow it as he wanted the money put in the bank. At the end of the war, Galicia was no longer part of the Austro-Hungarian Empire and was

14   Seefeldt, Fritz, H. Schweitzer, and J. Krämer, *Pfälzer Wandern: Kolonisation, Umsiedlung, Vertriebung, Heimkehr*, (Dornfelds Chronik II. Eutin: Struve's Buchdruckerei und Verlag, 1959).

ceded to Poland. The currency was so devalued that all they could buy with the money was a child's coat.

Mali attended the village school in Dornfeld, where there were eighty children assigned to one classroom and one teacher. She left school at the age of fourteen, was confirmed at Pentecost of 1922, and went on to help on the family farm. Although she was much smaller than her sister, Mali, she never had a problem milking cows or piling hay. She attended courses in the wintertime that were offered by the pastor, enjoyed dances (especially polkas and Viennese waltzes), singsongs, and other activities offered by the village church.

Amalie Schreyer was almost twenty years younger than Wilhelm Weber, but the two were married on June 19, 1928 in Dornfeld. He was a retired officer in the Austro-Hungarian Army whose first wife and child had died in childbirth. Wilhelm rented a small estate to farm near the town of Mykolaiv (Mikol'ajów) also known as Mikolaiv (Mikolajew), a Jewish town about fifteen kilometres south of Dornfeld. In March 1929, he brought Amalie to Dornfeld by horse and buggy as there was a midwife there. On April 29th she gave birth to Ella. She stayed in Dornfeld with her for another month.

Oberleutnant Wilhelm Weber, Austro-Hungarian Army WW1, 1917.

4.

Childhood in the '30s

"In the two largest European dictatorships (Germany and the Soviet Union), the war against the individual citizen started in the early 1930s, and in the Soviet Union that war was as costly in human lives as the later international conflict of World War Two. The impact of the Stalin terror on Soviet society was devastating."[15]

The Franz family of David and Elisabet and their three surviving children Käthe, Anna, and Johann (Hans) had relocated to Halbstadt in 1930 after the Nürnberg estate at Andreburg had been seized through collectivization by the Soviets. Hans's father David had obtained a position as manager of a bulk fuel storage facility. For two years (1933 to 1935) the family lived in Tiegenhagen, a small village four km south-west of Halbstadt. Hans entered school at the age of eight and completed the first and second grades in Tiegenhagen.

During the mid-1920s, many Mennonites considered leaving the Soviet Union. Years of turmoil (the First World War, the overthrow of the Tsar and civil war, the Bolshevik Revolution of 1917, banditry, and famine) had shaken many to the core. The "First Wave" of eighteen thousand Dutch Mennonites had left Russia in the 1870s for North America in response to the withdrawal of privileges (the introduction of universal military conscription) and the Russification policies of the Tsarist government. Between 1922 and 1928 another twenty-three thousand Mennonites emigrated to North America.

....

15   Epp, George K, *World War (1939-1945) - Soviet Union*, Global Anabaptist Mennonite
       Encyclopedia Online, 1989, last modified on March 10, 2019, at 01:52, https://gameo.org/index.
       php?title=World_War_(1939-1945)_-_Soviet_Union&oldid=163501.

Two of David Franz's siblings had left for Canada, his younger brother Peter in 1928 (who died in Saskatchewan in 1937) and a younger sister, Maria, who had married a Grunau and left for Canada in 1923 (Maria and her children resided in or near Waldheim, Saskatchewan). David Franz also wanted to emigrate, but Elisabet was hesitant. By 1929, the door for emigration was slammed shut.[16]

In addition to the Communist policies of collectivization and dekulakization[17] (agricultural landowners were declared to be kulaks or class enemies of the state), the Mennonites were undermined by laws like the following issued 8 April 1929 (as stated by Cornelius Krahn and Walter W. Sawatsky)[18]: "Religious organizations are forbidden to (a) organize mutual aid and co-operatives; (b) give material support to church members; (c) organize special meetings for children, youth, women, and prayer, and other meetings as well as general Bible literature, sewing societies, work groups and religious instruction groups, circles, and arrange for excursions and entertainment for children, for libraries and reading materials, and to organize hospitals and medical aid." Parents had to be very careful about what they said to their children about faith in God. My father said that, at the time, teachers at school would ask what was talked about in the home.

Famine also struck the land in the Soviet Union (and particularly Ukraine) in 1932-33, as a result of the Communist government's policies.[19] The first photo we have of our father dates from this period. He would have been seven or eight years old and is with his older sister Anna and their cousin Walter. They look hungry to me. My father told me of how they would glean in the fields for potatoes in the middle of the night (at two in the morning). Potatoes were the property of the state. He also would catch crayfish barehanded with his fingers in the Molotschnaya River. Another time he travelled at night alone on foot to the home of relatives in another village, looking for food. He knew the way and though his passage was noticed by barking dogs, he was never apprehended by any authorities.

16   Epp, Frank and Leo Driedger, *Mennonites*, The Canadian Encyclopedia, last modified on April 15, 2015, https://www.thecanadianencyclopedia.ca/en/article/mennonites.

17   Wikipedia, s.v. "Dekulakization," last modified on February 24, 2021, at 22:45 (UTC), https://en.wikipedia.org/wiki/Dekulakization.

18   Krahn, Cornelius and Walter W. Sawatsky, *Russia*, Global Anabaptist Mennonite Encyclopedia Online, February 2011, last modified on April 21, 2020, at 10:46, https://gameo.org/index.php?title=Russia&oldid=162227.

19   Wikipedia, s.v. "Soviet famine of 1932-33," last modified on February 26, 2021, at 16:19 (UTC), https://en.wikipedia.org/wiki/Soviet_famine_of_1932–33.

Johann Franz (R) with his sister Anna (L) and first cousin Walter Nürnberg 1933.

Sometime between 1936 and 1938, during the Great Purge[20], David Franz was arrested on the accusation that he had accepted a bribe (for what alleged purpose I don't know). My father said that his father had accepted a gift of a fowl (likely a goose) for Christmas and someone had informed on him. He spent months in prison but was one of only very few to be released. Most people arrested were executed or exiled.

Hans completed Grade Seven in 1940 and entered a marine technical school in Cherson (Kherson) on the Dnieper River (near the Black Sea port of Odessa) after successfully completing the entrance exam. Hans had ambitions to enter the merchant marine. That fall, free tuition was cut off. Hans's parents could not afford it themselves, so he returned home to Halbstadt and entered Grade Eight, which he completed in 1941.

Meanwhile, the Weber family of Wilhelm and Amalie with their daughter Ella lived on a rented estate near the Jewish town of Mikolajew (now known

....

20   Wikipedia, s.v. "The Great Purge," last modified on February 26, 2021, at 08:14 (UTC), https://
      en.wikipedia.org/wiki/Great_Purge.

as Mikolaiv), about fifteen kilometres south of Dornfeld.[21] Wilhelm was a successful farm manager, having owned numerous cows, bred horses, and fed many animals for slaughter with his brother on a large estate of six hundred "Joch" (eight hundred acres) near Popowce. When he married Amalie (Mali), it was the last year of a six year lease that he held on the larger estate. The smaller estate near Mikolajew was owned by the Catholic Church and was rented out by the priest. This land was in a very poor, rundown condition. Wilhelm improved the land so that they would have good crops and hay. They owned eight cows that provided "kosher" milk. Wilhelm loved horses, too, which seemed to obey him instantly.

Amalie, Willi, Ella and Wilhelm Weber 1934.

A son, Willi Friedrich, was born to Amalie and Wilhelm on January 17, 1932 in Mikolajew. The estate was now flourishing and the priest's sister decided to take it over. In the spring of 1933, Wilhelm and Amalie, along with four-year-old Ella and one-year-old Willi moved to Lemberg to open a small grocery store on Kostia Levytskoho Street. The family lived in an apartment on

....

21   Pawlosky, Nadia and Ella Franz, *They say overcoming adversity makes you stronger... Amalie Rupp is living proof,* school project, 2004.

Zelena Street, a block away. Milk was brought from Dornfeld, a twenty-five-kilometre journey, by horse and wagon seven days a week. The milk was not pasteurized and as people did not have refrigerators, the milk had to be boiled or left to sour to make yogurt. A baker brought buns twice a day to the store. They also carried coffee beans, raisins, and nuts. The business was successful and the family was reasonably well-off.

Wilhelm Weber 1935.

Ella Weber 1935.

On August 28, 1936, Amalie, Ella, and Willi were in Dornfeld for the 150th anniversary celebration of the emigration from the Rhine Palatinate. Wilhelm stayed in Lemberg to tend to the store. Not feeling well, he stepped outside to get some fresh air. He fell and hit his head on the stone step. Amalie rushed back to Lemberg by carriage but was not allowed to see him in the hospital. Wilhelm died later that day, likely from a stroke or heart attack. From that point on, Amalie then ran the store with the help of a clerk and a maid in the home. She had just managed to pay all the bills from the funeral, a year and a half later, when her son Willi fell ill. He died from complications of meningitis, measles, and an ear infection when he was just six years old, on February 16, 1938.

Amalie Weber (née Schreyer)/Johann Jakob Rupp wedding 1939.

Johann Jakob Rupp, a Mennonite, had been born in Krowica Sama, Poland on September 15, 1904 and was employed as a heavy duty mechanic by the Polish government. His parents Jakob Rupp and Maria Leise were originally from Falkenstein (near Dornfeld), the first Mennonite settlement of Galicia, which was founded in 1784 by seven Mennonite families from Falkenstein in the Palatinate, Germany. The Rupps were descended from Swiss Mennonites, perhaps from Mennonites in the Emmental area of the Canton of Bern, Switzerland, the original home of many of the Mennonite families of South Germany. At Easter, on April 9, 1939, Amalie married Johann Jakob (Hans) Rupp in the Lutheran Church on Zelena Street in Lemberg, adjacent to the apartment where she lived, by a Mennonite pastor.

5.

The Bombs Were falling on Lemberg: The Partition of Poland

On September 1, 1939, Poland was invaded by Nazi Germany. The German-Soviet non-aggression pact (Molotov-Ribbentrop Pact) had been signed in Moscow on August 23, 1939. The Soviet Union invaded Poland on September 17, 1939. The campaigns concluded in early October with Poland divided and annexed.

Lemberg was besieged by the German forces (the Wehrmacht and the Luftwaffe), starting on September 12. Ten-year-old Ella was staying with her grandparents in Dornfeld. She could see the bombs falling on Lemberg, where her mother Amalie and stepfather Johann Jakob were, and she was very afraid. Soviet forces arrived on September 19 and completed the encirclement of the city. Both German and Soviet envoys were negotiating with the Poles for the surrender of the city. Hitler decided on September 20 to leave the capture of the city to the Russians. The Polish commander General Sikorski decided the situation was hopeless and on September 22 the act of surrender was signed. Shortly after noon, the terms of surrender were broken when the NKVD (the Soviet secret police) began arresting all Polish officers. Most would be later murdered in the Katyn Massacre of 1940.[22]

....

22   Wikipedia, s.v. "Battle of Lwów (1939)," last modified on January 3, 2021, at 08:30 (UTC), https://en.wikipedia.org/wiki/Battle_of_Lwów_(1939).

When the Russians occupied Lemberg, Amalie closed her store and Johann Jakob left his work as a mechanic for the Polish government.

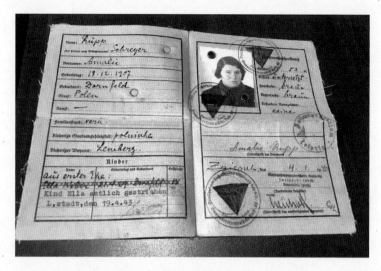

Deutsches Reich Rückkehrerausweis Amalie Rupp 1940.

Between December 24 and 27, 1939, the villagers of Dornfeld were relocated to the German occupation zone of the western part of Poland, to the Reichsgau Wartheland, also known as Warthegau.[23] On December 28, the Rupps were relocated from Lemberg by train to Łódź (renamed Litzmannstadt) and were registered nearby in Zgiersch (Zgierz) on January 4, 1940. Johann Jakob and Amalie were naturalized as German citizens (Volksdeutsche)[24] on January 4. His trade was recorded as locksmith. Amalie's mother Katherine had left Lemberg by train with the first group. She got very ill in the minus-thirty degrees Celsius temperatures and died of pneumonia and kidney failure in the relocation camp in Annaberg, Silesia at the age of fifty-six.

The Rupp family lived in a number of resettlement camps south and west of Leipzig (Lager Worbis in Thuringia for five months, Triptis, Bad Berka near Wilhelmsburg, and Rauschenberg).

....

23   Wikipedia, s.v. "Reichsgau Wartheland," last modified on January 6, 2021, at 17:10 (UTC), https://en.wikipedia.org/wiki/Reichsgau_Wartheland.

24   Wikipedia, s.v. "Volksdeutsche," last modified on February 15, 2021, at 16:13 (UTC), https://en.wikipedia.org/wiki/Volksdeutsche.

Personenbeschreibung Ella Weber 1943.

Their daughter Lydia was born in Buttstädt near Weimar (Thüringen) in August 1940 in a resettlement camp. Before being relocated back to Łódź on November 21, 1940, they stayed with Johann Jakob's sister in Pabrianice ten kilometres south-west of Łódź. In Łódź a friend found them a suite.

The Łódź Ghetto was the second-largest ghetto established by the Nazis. When Łódź was occupied by the German forces on September 8, 1939, the city had a population of 672 thousand people, of which over 230 thousand were Jewish. Polish and Jewish people were being evicted from their homes to make room for the ethnic Germans (Volksdeutsche) being relocated there. Polish people were displaced eastward, to the General Government area, also under German occupation and administration. The Jewish people were incarcerated in the ghetto, which was transformed into a major industrial centre for the manufacturing of war supplies. It was the last ghetto in occupied Poland to be closed, with the remaining population transported to Auschwitz and Chelmo extermination camps where most were murdered upon arrival. A total of 210 thousand Jewish people passed through the ghetto. About ten thousand of the Jewish residents of Łódź survived the Holocaust elsewhere.[25]

I knew nothing about the Łódź Ghetto until researching for this book. I knew that my mother's family had lived in Łódź for over four years. They had

....

25   Wikipedia, s.v. "Łódź Ghetto," last modified on February 14, 2021, at 23:59 (UTC), https://en.wikipedia.org/wiki/Łódź_Ghetto.

been resettled there as a consequence of the Hitler-Stalin pact to partition Poland. My grandmother did say that she knew there would be trouble, with people forcibly evicted from their homes to make way for the Volksdeutsche.

This revelation is actually more troubling for me than my father's war service in the Wehrmacht. I've had more time to process the latter, although I do reflect on it from time to time as I'm reminded of the atrocities of Nazi Germany. My family on both sides lost members to the war and my father was wounded and lamed. But in Łódź, my mother's family likely lived in the home of either Polish or Jewish civilians that had been forcibly evicted. Yes, they had lost their home and business in Lemberg and other family had lost their properties in Dornfeld. Other people now lived in their homes. But the situation my mother's family found themselves in is not comparable to those Polish civilians who were displaced to occupied territory or those Jewish civilians who were incarcerated in the ghetto and ultimately lost their lives in extermination camps.

My step-grandfather worked as a heavy duty mechanic maintaining and repairing German tanks (Panzers). So although he wasn't drafted into the Wehrmacht until late in the war, his work would have been considered an essential service and certainly benefitted the war effort.

On June 22, 1941, Nazi Germany launched Operation Barbarossa.[26] The goal was to conquer the western Soviet Union and repopulate it with Germans (Lebensraum). Some of the conquered would be used as slave labour, the rest were to be annihilated, and Germany would acquire the oil reserves of the Caucasus and the agricultural resources of the Soviet territories, primarily in Ukraine. This was the largest invasion force in the history of warfare and opened up the Eastern Front. The area saw some of World War Two's largest battles, highest casualties, and most horrific atrocities. It changed the course of the war. The Third Reich could not sustain the effort which took its forces to the gates of Moscow at the end of 1941, and the Soviet winter counter-offensive pushed them back. Eventually the Wehrmacht had to retreat after the Battle of Stalingrad[27] in 1943 and the force collapsed.

....

26 Wikipedia, s.v. " Operation Barbarossa," last modified on February 27, 2021, at 09:07 (UTC), https://en.wikipedia.org/wiki/Operation_Barbarossa.

27 Wikipedia, s.v. "Battle of Stalingrad," last modified on February 26, 2021, at 07:35 (UTC), https://en.wikipedia.org/wiki/Battle_of_Stalingrad.

6.

Papa's Life Story

From Johann Franz's own account (translation from German completed by the author):

"*In 1941, after Johann had come home and entered Grade Eight after tuition at the naval training centre in Kherson he attended was no longer free and his parents could no longer support him, the German-Russian War began.*

He applied for an apprenticeship as a locksmith in Saporoshje, near Chortitza. Along with his peers, he was assigned to a bench, but they no longer came to study their craft. Instead, one day the whole school was assigned to dig trenches to stop the German Panzer tanks and was sent to a field outside the city. Unfortunately, the organizers forgot to provide the students with food and water and there were no spades available. As he learned that the school was about to be evacuated to Krasnodar, he contacted his father to ask what to do: whether to go with the school or to come home. To travel to Krasnodar was a distance of about seven hundred kilometres. His father said to come home as they were to be relocated anyway — at least this way, they'd be together as a family. The next day he came home without the necessary travel papers and did not register his whereabouts with the authorities as required.

Every now and then, people went from house to house looking for men and boys to go digging trenches, but Johann would keep watch and disappear through the garden when they did. In his last days in his hometown, he left the house only after dark. His father worked in the village of Heidelberg, twenty kilometres from Halbstadt, in the shop. Eventually, he was sent from there with the men to the east.

On the 5th of September, 1941 Johann's father came home by bicycle to say goodbye. That was the last time they saw each other.

The front came closer and closer. At the end of September, an NKVD officer came into the house and read the family the petition. He let them know about their evacuation to Kazakhstan, and registered Johann's mother and sister Gretel for deportation. In the afternoon the officer came back to the house. Johann's mother said he had just come home and asked if he could go with them. When asked how old he was, his mother said fifteen (a year younger than he really was). If she had truthfully said he was sixteen, Johann would likely have been deported into forced labour or conscripted into the Soviet army.

The next day, a Russian soldier with a mounted bayonet on a loaded rifle came over and took them to a transit camp near the police station. Many people from Halbstadt were already there. Others were near the train station. The front was rapidly approaching. German planes were dropping bombs on Halbstadt. The family was strictly guarded by soldiers. On the morning of October 4, hearing the approaching machine gunfire, the last Russian soldiers withdrew.

Johann went home and got the trolley for the family's things. Together they left the camp. At eleven o'clock, they learned the Germans were already in the centre of Halbstadt. Two weeks later, he registered as an interpreter. An officer (doctor) picked him up with his driver. Wanting to say goodbye to his mother, he met her on the street in front of their house.

He was assigned to a field hospital of a mountain division. With this unit, he travelled to the Caucasus. After the German defeat at Stalingrad, they were in danger of being cut off and the Caucasus army retreated across the Straits of Kerch to the Crimea. From there, they were transferred by rail over Romania and Bulgaria, to Yugoslavia. They ultimately landed in Greece. Then the German retreat began.

In 1944, Johann and other younger comrades of his from the field hospital were dispatched to a field replacement battalion. They were posted as messengers to battalion staff. Here, Johann heard interpreters were being sought again, specifically those who were able to speak Russian. He applied and was transferred to a higher staff.

In Yugoslavia, Johann was wounded by a low-flying aircraft shortly before the end of the war and was evacuated to Austria. From there, he moved to Backnang, Germany, where he would meet his future wife, Ella Weber, and ultimately emigrate to Canada in 1949."

7.

The "Trudarmee", Forced Labour and Deportation

The "Trudarmee", also known as the "Arbeitsarmee", was a system of forced labour run by the Soviet Union from 1941 to 1946, primarily for Russians of German descent—initially for men between the ages of sixteen to sixty. Later, in October of 1942, women between sixteen and forty-five—save for those who were pregnant or had children under the age of three—were conscripted to the program, too.

Labourers were accommodated in barracks surrounded by barbed wire under military guard. Food rations were established as the norm of the Gulag, the government agency in charge of the Soviet forced-labour camp system.[28] No contact with civilians without the express authorization of the authorities was permitted. Unauthorized departures from the designated location was considered to be desertion and punished accordingly.[29,30]

The total number of German forced labourers was around 350 thousand for the duration of the war. Eighty to 90 percent of the men and about a third of the women were interned in forced labour camps. Death rates in the camps were high (at least 20 percent) and the toll on families, especially children,

---

28   Wikipedia, s.v. "Gulag," last modified on February 27, 2021, at 07:03 (UTC), https://en.wikipedia.org/wiki/Gulag.

29   Trudarmee - Zwangsarbeitslager - 1, *Geschichte der Deutschen aus Russland*, accessed March 13, 2021, https://deutscheausrussland.de/2017/03/08/trudarmee-1/.

30   Trudarmee - Zwangsarbeitslager - 2, *Geschichte der Deutschen aus Russland*, accessed March 13, 2021, https://deutscheausrussland.de/2017/03/27/trudarmee-zwangsarbeitslager-ii/.

was immense. It is estimated that 50 percent of the Mennonite men in the Molotschna perished. The loss of life was also high among the evacuated women and children.[31]

Johann's father David, David's brother Nikolaus (Klas) and brother-in-law Hans Nürnberg were all drafted into forced labour and deported to Siberia on the far side of the Ural Mountains. As my father's account goes, he narrowly avoided the same fate.

Johann had avoided Stalin's 1941 draft of the German men into forced labour, but as the Soviet authorities prepared to evacuate the women and children of Halbstadt eastwards, his mother prevailed on him to go with her and his younger sister. Though Johann "surfaced" when he reported to the holding area near the police station, along with his mother and his sister, for evacuation, this never came to fruition. The Soviets managed to evacuate about a third of the remaining residents of Halbstadt before the German advance reached it, but not the three remaining family members. Two weeks later, sixteen-year-old Johann volunteered with the Wehrmacht as an interpreter.

Johann's father David left a letter[32] to his family (transcribed by Johann and translated from German by the author):

"24.3.44
Meljutino

Dear loved ones!

Dear wife and children, dear Ännchen, Hans, and Gretel. Since I feel I will not live much longer, I want to share something with you, dear ones. Our farewell was brief at the time. Who thought that it would be forever? Now, as God wills it, if not here, we will see ourselves in the next world, if an afterlife exists, again. Man does not gamble away his life if he believes . . . we are still being built up. We came in 2 camps, I was put in 3 Rayon, brother Klas and brother-in-law Hans were put in 2 Rayon, which were 3 km apart. In each camp housed between 4½ and 5 thousand men, all Germans

31   Trudarmee - Zwangsarbeitslager - 2.

32   It is not known where the original letter might be.

*from all over Ukraine. Later on, Volga-Germans[33] were added. The food was
initially quite good. We regularly got bread, fish, cheese, butter. We still had
food from home that we had left; we were not suffering. The camp rations also
started well at the beginning. Then the rations became smaller. Production
standards were set and food given according to them. Bread was reduced from
5 kilos to 1. And the quality of the soup declined. The further we got into
the winter, the worse the climatic conditions became. The cold—minus 40-50
degrees—the weak clothes. We got rough clothing, boots, gloves, cotton trou-
sers and jackets, and underwear. My shoes were completely broken when I
arrived. In the hurry from Heidelberg I had forgotten my galoshes—the new
ones I had from Hans. On the bed, I left the blanket there, too. You probably
were never able to return either. I'm sorry I did not come to Halbstadt again.
Then, maybe, I could have stayed home. If they had shot me, I would not have
had to go through all this. The worst is to starve. Because now, there are no
prospects; I am unable to work, and they gave me the bread ration of only 200
grams a day, nothing more. The local population cannot help us all. In a word
for the Germans that were here and in the surrounding area the last song is
sung, many are already no more, some struggle on, but to the harvest is still 5
months away.*

*Now, back to Solikamsk. There, I worked through October and November,
before the commission declared me as 100% invalid, and not suited to work
anymore. My bread ration was increased to 400 grams. I lived like this for
a month, before being called to work, where invalids received 500 grams of
bread. I then was assigned to heating the stove, as night watchman; that
was hard, too. Then, our Naradschik[34] came to the barracks and asked, "Do
you want to work in the office?" I accepted right away. I went to the cater-
ing department. The accountant was friendly, a good person who liked me,
who gave me the responsibility to sew things, as I was without salary. For the
sewing, I got paid and also had to meet production targets. I overachieved by
180-200%, and so would get 800-900 grams of bread, three bowls of soup in
the morning and evening, and, for lunch, a thick gruel. There, I worked till*

33   University of Alberta, *The Volga Germans*, https://sites.ualberta.ca/~german/AlbertaHistory/
      Volgagermans.htm. Volga Germans were the descendants of Germans that had left their homeland to
      settle in the Volga valley, at the invitation of the Russian Tsarina Catherine in 1763.

34   Naradschyk is the Ukrainian word for counsellor.

April, at which point all invalids, weak ones, were let go. Everyone had to give an address where he had relatives in Siberia, where he was allowed to go. I had Ella's address and also my sister-in-law Schnura's. I committed myself to go to Ella. They lived tolerably, trading clothes for food, because the ration (Pajak[35]) was not quite enough. I'll now describe the journey from Solikamsk to here. About 3 weeks before we left the camp, I became swollen, my legs so heavy, I could not walk. My body was so swollen that I could not breathe. I could not eat, but not for lack of hunger—it was said to be Zinga[36]. The doctor gave me a powder, but the doctors did not want to make much effort with the weak, as they were dismissed as invalids.

I was acquainted with a Feldscher[37], one of us Germans, who worked in the ambulance. I promised him my food, because I could not eat, he should help me. He brought me a ½ litre bottle of green liquid 3 times a day. He said the swelling would subside in 5 days, and so it was. By the time of my departure, I was restored. The camp was suffering from an epidemic disease, the red dysentery, which has plagued many people. I was always afraid of being affected. And the last day before we were to leave, I got the diarrhea. But I did not go to the doctor—this would mean being held back. I could only go on, to freedom. On the way, we found 700 grams of bread and 5 cans of peas. I then kept quite a diet because of the diarrhea. We arrived at the station called Brede. It was melting weather, cold at night. There was no boiled water to drink. But, in the morning, I was so thirsty, I went to the Wodokachka[38] and drank heavily on my empty stomach. I then went to the Peron[39]; there, a woman sold sauerkraut. I was so hungry that I bought a saucer and ate it all, and my diarrhea was gone. Now we were at Brede, 110 km from Sovchos[40], all water outside, our footwear was falling apart. We were at Brede for 9 days, but there was nothing you could buy with money, and we had nothing to trade. Then, we relied on begging for whatever the Russians would give us. We were

35   Pajak is the Russian word for ration.
36   Johann Franz described Zinga as beriberi, a disease caused by a vitamin B-1 deficiency, also known as thiamine deficiency.
37   Johann Franz described a Feldscher as a medic.
38   Wodokachka is the Russian word for pump-house.
39   Johann Franz translated this from Ukrainian as Bahnsteig, which is German for platform.
40   Sovkhoz is the Russian word for a state-owned farm.

9 men, and some had food left. I had nothing, so I bought from the others. We also bought supplies on the way. We left Brede on foot; there was no other possibility. We were 4 men, a Janzen, Görtzen from Franztal, a man from Landskrone. The first day, we got wet, because of heavy rain. On the way was a Kyrgyz[41] house, a cattle herder's, where we rented a room. It was so crowded that we had to sleep in the hallway, but there was, fortunately, a Pliet[42], which we could light. We laid ourselves down with the wet clothes and rested as well as was possible. In the morning, we went on to Kolchos Kusakan. We had 75 km to go, then; it was time to beg again, the people were stingy, had gotten little. It was threshing time, so they said we could help thresh. But then we got so much together until the next station. There, we went to the next kolchos, but there were loud Kyrgyz. Nobody wanted to keep us overnight; no headman was at home. Thankfully, a militia officer put us up. There was no hope of finding bread or food. We made do with what we had. On the way, Görtzen told he could no longer keep pace with us, only follow slowly; he was still suffering from diarrhea. We then made a pilgrimage for three. We then arrived at Kolchos Kusakan before evening. There, we met the first Germans from Ukraine we had encountered, from the Volga. There were questions back and forth and they fed us, as the Volga Germans still had grain from home. We got milk Airan[43]. We had not drunk milk for a long time. We all also tasted coffee, of course. We then spent 2 days resting, them providing us with food, before continuing on our way. We covered 18-20 km that day, as we were not able to do more.

In Kusakan, we learned that our travel cohort, Görtzen, had sat down on the way and FALLEN asleep forever. I'm not sure what happened to him; who knows if he was buried or if the wolves took pity . . . ."

David and Nikolaus Franz, and David's brother-in-law, Hans Nürnberg, were in adjoining labour camps near Solikamsk. Solikamsk is in the Perm Krai of Russia, and there were a number of Gulag camps in the Perm, as there were in other parts of the Soviet Union.[44] Solikamsk is more than 1,000 km north of

---

41   Johann Franz thought these might be Kazakhs.

42   Pliet is the Russian word for stove.

43   Airan is a Turkish drink made from sour milk.

44   Wikipedia, s.v. "List of Gulag camps," last modified on February 2, 2021, at 16:22 (UTC), https://en.wikipedia.org/wiki/List_of_Gulag_camps.

Brede, Chelyabinsk Oblast, near Kazakhstan. Upon David's release in March of
1944 because of illness, he and other invalids also released must have traveled by
train in a southerly direction until they reached Brede, from where they could
only travel on foot. David managed to walk about a hundred kilometres to the
home of relatives in Milyutinka (Meljutino), Kazakhstan. He shared a bed with
one of the children and, one morning, the boy appeared and said "*Onkel David
ist kalt*" (Uncle David is cold). David died on April 15, 1944. Johann's mother,
Elisabet, received the news of her husband's fate in 1972 from relatives, more
than thirty years after he had been conscripted into forced labour.

Another account was related by my father's second cousin, Warkentin (Ken)
Schroeter of Poulsbo, Washington. His article is entitled "One Day in the Life
of Ivan Nikolaevich".[45] Warkentin invited my father to accompany him and his
wife on a journey to Siberia in the late 1990s, in search of a mutual cousin, but
my father was reluctant to do so, as he had left the Soviet Union illegally in
World War II. I have letters to my father from both Ken Schroeter, in English,
and his first cousin, Ivan Nikolaevich Franz, in Russian.

"ONE DAY IN THE LIFE OF IVAN NIKOLAEVICH,
by Warkentin Schroeter

*"The eleven-year-old boy peeks out through a crack in the wall of a box-car
that he and his family had been packed into, along with dozens of other ethnic
Germans who had not retreated with the German army when their advances
into the Soviet Union had faltered and failed, looking out over the rolling
hills that are called the Ural Mountains, on their way deep into Siberia.
His grandparents had managed to escape into Germany, but his father,
Nikolai Franz, had decided to stick it out in the Soviet Union because they
had known a good life there. Now they were on their way to a labor camp
to work the coal mines around Anzhero-Sudzhensk near the dividing line
between western Siberia and eastern Siberia. The camp was close to where the
rest of the family were detained, and so communications could continue. But
after their communications had stopped, the family learned that Nikolai had
died from overwork and starvation.*

45   Warkentin Schroeter, One Day in the Life of Ivan Nikolaevich, Poulsbo, Washington, USA, 2000.

"Johann was now thirteen years old. He was finishing his schooling where the Russian language and Soviet culture were emphasized. While most ethnic Germans in this situation shunned the overt Soviet indoctrination, Johann chose to adapt. For this he was a disappointment to his mother and his older sister who was in an advanced state of tuberculosis. Johann went so far as to adopt the Russian form of his name, Ivan, and even more to marry a Russian girl who already had one child, a son. Now he became estranged from his family. He remained, nevertheless, a handsome and spirited lad and Evdokia was undeniably a pretty lass. His mother, Mrs. Alexandra Trenkenschu Franz (who was also my father's cousin), and her infirm daughter, Elvira, both died months apart leaving young Ivan without a family."

He writes that he and his wife Birgit *"were planning a trip through Siberia with a stopover in Itat where we hoped to at least see and shake hands with my second cousin, the last known survivor on the Schroeter-Vogt side of our family in Russia, even if we couldn't communicate otherwise, having almost no command of the Russian language ourselves, and he knowing absolutely no English.... To our utter delight, he could recall enough of his childhood German to converse with us, although his sentences often drifted into and ended in Russian.... But after lunch we both pulled out our family pictures. We also brought family pictures from the Johann Franz family, a first cousin in Canada."*

8.

The Wehrmacht

The Wehrmacht was the unified armed forces of Nazi Germany from 1935 to 1945. After the Nazi rise to power in 1933, Adolf Hitler established the Wehrmacht as a modern offensive military force to fulfill the Nazi regime's long-term goals of regaining lost territory and gaining new territory. In the early part of World War II, the Wehrmacht employed combined arms tactics (air-support, tanks, and infantry) in what became known as "Blitzkrieg." This early success often found the rapidly advancing troops far ahead of the necessary support of the supply lines. Nevertheless, historians have generally understood the Wehrmacht as one of the most powerful fighting forces in history. Of course, the Wehrmacht was a horrifying enterprise, complicit, as it was, in conjunction with the SS and Waffen-SS, in the Holocaust, as well as war crimes in Greece and Yugoslavia.[46]

One book in particular stands out on this topic: Hermann Frank Meyer's *Bloody Edelweiss, the First Mountain Division in the Second World War (Blutiges Edelweiss, Die 1. Gebirgs-Division im Zweiten Weltkrieg).*[47] The edelweiss, worn on cap and sleeve, was the division badge of the First Mountain Division of the Wehrmacht, the elite Nazi force for which Johann would volunteer.

....

46   Wikipedia, s.v. "Wehrmacht," last modified on February 14, 2021, at 19:21 (UTC), https://en.wikipedia.org/wiki/Wehrmacht.

47   Meyer, Hermann Frank, *Blutiges Edelweiss, Die 1. Gebirgs-Division im 2. Weltkrieg* (Berlin: Christof Links Verlag GmbH, 2008).

As part of the Wehrmacht, the First Mountain Division[48] invaded Poland in 1939 and reached Lemberg, where the Battle of Lwów took place.[49] The division took part in the Battle of France in May and June of 1940, during which German forces occupied France, Belgium, Luxembourg, and the Netherlands.[50] The division was selected to be part of planned operations against the United Kingdom and Gibraltar, which were subsequently cancelled. The division then took part in the invasion of Yugoslavia by German, Italian, and Hungarian forces in April 1941.[51]

The First Mountain Division participated in the invasion of the Soviet Union when Operation Barbarossa was launched on June 22, 1941. The Wehrmacht reached Lemberg (Lwów) in eight days. Prior to the arrival of the German forces, there was an uprising of Ukrainian nationalists against the Soviet regime on June 25 and 26, in anticipation of relief from their oppressors. There were harsh reprisals by the Soviet secret police, the NKVD. Upon arrival of the Wehrmacht, the citizenry suffered another blow, an equally harsh pogrom of Jewish residents.

By early September 1941, the First Mountain Division had engaged in three major battles with Soviet forces, the first near Jaroslau, Poland, in the latter part of June. The second major battle had been at Winniza in Ukraine, in late July, after they had pushed through the "Stalin-Linie," a line of fortifications—concrete bunkers and gun emplacements.[52] The third major battle had taken place at Uman-Podwyssokoje, east of Winniza, in early August. The First Mountain Division had then headed southeast to Berislaw (near Cherson on the Black Sea), before turning northeast, toward Tokmak, in early September. They then had to cross the defensive works of the "Panzergraben" near Timoschewka: anti-tank ditches constructed by labourers conscripted by the Soviets to encumber the advance of German tanks (Panzers).

48   Wikipedia, s.v. "1st Mountain Division (Wehrmacht)," last modified on January 17, 2021, at 16:17 (UTC), https://en.wikipedia.org/wiki/1st_Mountain_Division_(Wehrmacht).

49   Wikipedia, s.v. "Battle of Lwów," last modifed on March 8, 2021, at 04:39 (UTC), https://en.wikipedia.org/wiki/Battle_of_Lwów_(1939).

50   Wikipedia, s.v. "Battle of France," last modified on March 4, 2021, at 23:21 (UTC), https://en.wikipedia.org/wiki/Battle_of_France.

51   Wikipedia, s.v. "Invasion of Yugoslavia," last modified on March 5, 2021, at 16:12 (UTC), https://en.wikipedia.org/wiki/Invasion_of_Yugoslavia.

52   Wikipedia, s.v. "Stalin Line," last modified on November 21, 2020, at 16:58 (UTC), https://en.wikipedia.org/wiki/Stalin_Line.

On October 4, 1941, the Wehrmacht reached Halbstadt, and the remaining residents awaiting deportation at the train station were able to return to their homes. Two weeks later, Johann volunteered with the Wehrmacht's First Mountain Division as a translator and was assigned to a Field Hospital unit. When he volunteered, on October 17, 1941, he was issued a German uniform with the national emblem, a breast eagle, to wear. He later received a draft notice and was officially conscripted on January 1, 1942.

The battle at Tokmak raged in early October. In his memoirs[53], Hubert Lanz, the general in command of the First Mountain Division in the Eastern Europe campaign (and later, the Twenty-Second Mountain Army Corps) stated in German (as translated by the author): "Over a hundred thousand prisoners, as well as numerous guns and tanks had fallen into German hands. The Russian 18th Army is worn out. The First Mountain Division has a decisive share in this great success".[54]

Cumulative losses for the First Mountain Division since the launch of Operation Barbarossa on June 22 were 160 officers, 700 non-commissioned officers, and 3,700 enlisted men. The division was hoping to relocate to Crimea, but instead were ordered by high command to march northeast to Stalino (Donezk or Donetsk) and then southeast to Taganrog to overwinter along the Mius River near the Sea of Azov.

The winter of 1941-2 was harsh, with cold temperatures of minus-thirty degrees Celsius and deep snow, conditions for which the Wehrmacht troops were poorly clad. On January 20, 1942, the Red Army launched a winter offensive against the German forces and on February 18, most of the mountain troops were withdrawn to march northwest toward Barwenkowo.

All enlisted men received a service medal commemorating the "Winterschlacht im Osten 1941/42" (the "Winter Campaign in the East 1941/42"). Johann traded his medal for a loaf of bread with another soldier, thinking that surviving the winter was no big deal for him as he lived there. Later, he had second thoughts and traded his cigarette ration with another soldier to get the medal back.

At Easter, 1942, Johann received a pass to see his mother and sister. In a letter from my grandmother to my father, dated June 5, 1956, after fourteen

....

53 Lanz, Hubert, *Gebirgsjäger, Die 1. Gebirgsdivision 1935-1945* (Bad Nauheim, 1954), 149.

54 Meyer, *Blutiges Edelweiss*, 72.

years without any contact from him or knowledge of his whereabouts, she wrote, "Well, I'm so happy, so thankful, Hans. I felt as happy as Easter 1942, when you, who I believed to be dead, stood before me. Yes, there is still joy in our lives. Thank God for that!"

The major battle at Barwenkowo began on May 17 and lasted ten days, with two armies of the Soviet Union destroyed and 240 thousand Soviet prisoners taken. The division lost 190 officers and enlisted men, had 417 wounded, and seven missing in action.

On June 22, 1942 (the anniversary of the launch of Operation Barbarossa), the summer offensive began. The objective was to cross the Caucasus Mountains and capture the strategic oilfields. The Mountain troops were to take the high passes. On August 25, the Red Army launched a counter-attack. This was one occasion where Johann had a close call, as a Soviet plane flew over the top of the pass that the German forces were ascending and strafed them with machine-gun fire. Although the campaign lasted until December, the Wehrmacht was ultimately driven back.

Yugoslavia had been invaded by Axis forces on April 6, 1941 and partitioned between Germany, Italy, Hungary, Bulgaria and puppet regimes. Subsequently, a guerrilla liberation war and a multi-side civil war was fought by Yugoslav Partisans. The human cost of the war was enormous, including numerous reprisal actions against civilians for resistance activity.[55]

Greece had been invaded from Albania by the Italians on October 28, 1940. The Greeks launched a counteroffensive on November 14. After the Italians ran into difficulty, the Germans began their attack on April 6, 1941. The First Mountain Division was sent to Greece in June 1943 and returned to Yugoslavia in November of the same year.

Italy capitulated to the Allies on September 3 and, on October 13, declared war on Nazi Germany.[56] Following the Italian surrender in September, the Wehrmacht committed the Massacre of the Acqui Division [57] on the Greek

55   Wikipedia, s.v. "World War II in Yugoslavia," last modified on February 16, 2021, at 15:23 (UTC), https://en.wikipedia.org/wiki/World_War_II_in_Yugoslavia.

56   Oct. 13, 1943 Italy Switches Sides in World War II, *The New York Times*, https://learning.blogs. nytimes.com/2011/10/13/oct-13-1943-italy-switches-sides-in-world-war-ii/, accessed April 11, 2020.

57   Wikipedia, s.v. "Massacre of the Acqui Division," last modified on March 6, 2021, at 22:01 (UTC), https://en.wikipedia.org/wiki/Massacre_of_the_Acqui_Division.

island of Cephalonia. The massacre which served as the basis of the book and film Captain Corelli's Mandolin,[58] was one of the largest prisoner-of-war massacres of the war.

The First Mountain Division was sent to Albania and on to Greece again in May 1944, returning to Yugoslavia in July, where they spent the remainder of the war. On May 7, 1945, the chief-of-staff of the German Armed Forces High Command, General Alfred Jodi, signed a document of unconditional surrender to the Allies, on behalf all German forces.[59]

I wrote to the Deutsche Dienststelle (WASt)[60] to inquire about my father's military records. The records of military personnel in both World Wars have now been moved under the authority of the German Federal Archives in Koblenz. Translated from its original German (see the Appendix), it reads, "Your father's personal papers (military passport, military log, and personnel file) are not available here; they have probably been lost in the war. For this reason, it is not possible to provide complete proof of his service. The following is confirmed from other documents of the former Wehrmacht:

"FRANZ, Johann, born on 24.02.1925 in Andreburg / Ukraine

Home Address:	1944	Mother: Elisabeth Franz, Halbstadt / Ukraine Goethe Street 5
Identification Tag:	-96-	F. Laz. Geb. Brig. (Mountain Brigade Field Hospital)
Troops:		
on	06.02.1944	Field Hospital 54 (motorized) *Subordination: 1. Mountain Division Operational area: Croatia *)*

....

58   Wikipedia, s.v. "Captain Corelli's Mandolin (film)," last modified on January 4, 2021, at 13:46 (UTC), https://en.wikipedia.org/wiki/Captain_Corelli's_Mandolin_(film).

59   Wikipedia, s.v. "End of World War II in Europe," last modified on February 23, 2021, at 09:06 (UTC), https://en.wikipedia.org/wiki/End_of_World_War_II_in_Europe.

60   Wikipedia, s.v. "Deutsche Dienststelle (WASt)," last modified on May 9, 2020, at 17:50 (UTC), https://en.wikipedia.org/wiki/Deutsche_Dienststelle_(WASt).

from	07.02.1944)	4th Company Field Replacement Battalion 654
and on	11.04.1944)	
from	11.04.1944)	2nd Company Field Replacement Battalion 654
and on	20.09.1944)	*The Field Replacement Battalion 654 was under the 104. Jäger Division.* *Operational area: February-September 1944 West Greece *)*

The above records show that Johann was part of the Ninety-Sixth Mountain Brigade Field Hospital. On February 6, 1944, Johann served in Croatia in a motorized Field Hospital unit (the Fifty-Fourth Field Medical Battalion). He was then transferred to the Fourth Company Field Replacement Battalion 654 on February 7. On April 4, he was transferred to the Second Company Field Replacement Battalion 654, subordinate of the 104th Jäger Division, posted to the western part of Greece.

Gebirgsjäger were the light infantry who were part of the alpine or mountain troops (the Gebirgstruppe) of Germany, Austria, and Switzerland.[61] I have my father's brigade identification tag (or "dog tag") and "Soldbuch"—his paybook and identity papers—though they are a copy, in his case. My father explained he had had a copy made in order to remove any reference to his country of origin (Ukraine, which was part of the Soviet Union). His birthplace is simply listed as Andreburg, which could easily be in any German-speaking land. The copy is dated March 4, 1945. It shows his rank as "Obergefreiter" (corporal or lance corporal) and records the serial numbers of a gas mask and series of weapons issued to him. According to his Soldbuch, he was issued a Gewehr 33/40, "a bolt-action rifle, sometimes considered a carbine, used exclusively by

....

61   Wikipedia, s.v. "Gebirgsjäger," last modified on February 19, 2021, at 04:42 (UTC), https:// en.wikipedia.org/wiki/Gebirgsjäger.

Germany's elite mountain troops, the Gebirgsjäger,"[62] on August 8, 1943. On May 15, 1944, he was issued a "Seitengewehr Säbel," a bayonet. On October 25, 1944, he was issued a pistol—specifically, a Pistole Model 27 or P27,[63] which, according to my father, was overdue, issued, for self-protection, some time after enlistment.

A certificate issued to him dated June 8, 1945, states that he was wounded on April 13, 1945, and subsequently awarded a "Verwundetenabzeichen in Schwarz"[64] ("badge of the wounded in black"), the equivalent of an American purple heart. I have not seen this badge and it has likely gone missing. Either that, or my father perhaps received the award as certificate only (and had it recorded in his Soldbuch). I have also seen his medical records book, which goes into detail about his wounds, but this document has likewise gone missing, presumably packed away somewhere.

My father briefly mentioned this award when he came to visit us the year he died. We were sitting in the backyard in the sun, when he gave me his Soldbuch, brigade identification tag, and service medal. He also brought a book he had recently acquired, Helmet T. Huebert's *Molotschna Historical Atlas*. He told us he had been brows-

Johann Franz's Wehrmacht Soldbuch and assorted memorabilia WW2.

ing through the book and read the section on Halbstadt and was surprised to find his name in there. He exclaimed: "I never thought I would find myself in a book!"

My father told me it was when he had just finished his shift, sleeping under a tree outside a field hospital, when a low-flying Soviet plane came and bombed it. He caught some shrapnel in his back—a minor flesh wound—but lost a good

62   Wikipedia, s.v. "Gewehr 33/40," https://world-war-2.wikia.org/wiki/Gewehr_33/40, accessed March 9, 2021.

63   Wikipedia, s.v. "ČZ vz. 27," last modified on February 15, 2021, at 21:00 (UTC), https://en.wikipedia.org/wiki/ČZ_vz._27.

64   Wikipedia, s.v. "Verwundetenabzeichen (1939),", last modified on October 20, 2020, at 15:49, https://de.wikipedia.org/wiki/Verwundetenabzeichen_(1939).

chunk of the muscle of his inner left thigh, near the groin. A nerve had also been shot through in his right leg. Doctors tried to reconnect it but were unsuccessful. My father said he was given the choice of staying put or being transported to Austria by hospital train and, as the Yugoslav partisans weren't taking any prisoners, he chose to be evacuated (though the hospital train he boarded was to come under fire several times, too).The Soldbuch records that Johann was in the local hospital on April 18, transferred to a hospital train on April 20, and then to several reserve and field hospitals thereafter. The last date stamp on that page is August 3, 1945.

Johann came to convalesce in a military hospital in Linz, Austria which was under American occupation. His wound on his upper thigh eventually healed and a number of skin grafts were employed, but the thinness of the skin over the wound gave him occasional grief for the rest of his life. He had to learn to walk again. He walked with a limp. My sister Margaret asked our father how the mood was in the hospital, among the wounded German soldiers. He said it was good; everyone was just happy to have survived the war. The last date stamp in the Soldbuch is August 14, 1947, in English: "No. 2 Sep Documentation Unit", which must have stamped by the American administration.

My father walked out of that hospital in the fall of 1947, pretending to have papers (he patted his breast pocket) and into freedom. He had his German uniform altered by a local tailor to resemble the national Austrian dress. He had heard there were people from his area in the refugee camp at Backnang, Germany (near Stuttgart) and so he made his way there in October of 1947. He was afraid that he would fall into Soviet hands as Austria was under joint occupation of the Allies and divided into four zones (French, American, British, and Soviet). He must have travelled by train to Germany, a distance of about 500 kilometres, all in the American zone.

9.

The Great Trek of 1943-1945

The Wehrmacht capitulated to the Soviet army at the Battle of Stalingrad, the turning point of the war on the Eastern Front. In the summer of 1943, the Wehrmacht was ordered to retreat and to take with it the remaining population of Soviet Germans. These numbered some 350,000 civilians of which about 35,000 were Mennonites.[65]

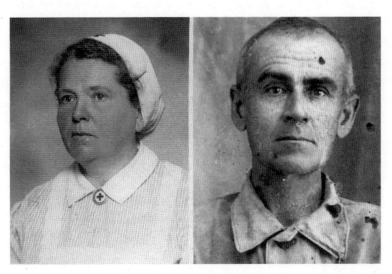

Elisabet Franz, nurse in Hohensalza (Inowroclaw, Poland) 1944, David Franz 1941.

....

65   Huebert, Helmut T. and Susan Huebert, *Great Trek, 1943-1945*, Global Anabaptist Mennonite Encyclopedia Online, April 2009, last modified November 23, 2017, at 07:17, https://gameo.org/index.php?title=Great_Trek,_1943-1945&oldid=155816.

In the Molotschna, word was received on September 9 and 10 by the mayors of the Mennonite villages that they should obtain wagons for every family. Over the next two days, a caravan of wagons stretching ten kilometres long set out to the southwest. Refugees from the Chortitza Mennonite settlement joined in late September and people from the Zagradovka Mennonite settlement in late October. Travelling by horse and wagon, on foot, or on trains, they reached the Warthegau area west of Warsaw by the middle of March of 1944. As most of the able-bodied men had already been murdered or exiled, the fragmented families consisted of mainly women, old men, and children. Johann's mother, Elisabet, and eleven-year-old younger sister, Gretel, were among them. Many people had died of disease along the way or were killed by the Soviets or local partisans. Johann's older sister, Anna Volk, and her children also fled to Poland. Anna passed away from illness in November 1944 and her children were taken in by others with their whereabouts unknown.

The Soviet advance continued and, by January 18, 1945, had reached Poland and East Prussia. The resulting evacuation was a disorganized scramble further westward. Many refugees were killed in the Soviet advance and the aircraft bombing and strafing of refugee columns. It is not known how far west my paternal grandmother and aunt managed to reach, but it was almost certainly short of the Elbe River, the dividing line between east and west as agreed on in Yalta. Stalin had insisted to Churchill and Roosevelt at the Yalta Conference of February 1945 that all Soviet citizens be returned to the Soviet Union, willingly or otherwise.[66] My aunt Gretel's future husband, Adam Mündt, would later recount that his family had only one more bridge to cross, but the way was blocked by the Red Army. Elisabet and her youngest child, Gretel, were thereby "repatriated" to Siberia in 1946. Elisabet died March 16, 1975, in Novosibirsk, Siberia.

A couple of stories were related to me by my aunt, Tante Gretel Mündt, when we visited her in Germany in 2008. One such story is set in Poland, I believe, in 1945, after the end of the war. Oma Elisabet Franz and Tante Gretel were in a camp somewhere where the men's barracks were separated from those of the women and children. At night, she told us, the women and children

66   Fitzpatrick, Sheila, "The Motherland Calls: "Soft" Repatriation of Soviet Citizens from Europe, 1945-1953," *The Journal of Modern History*, Volume 90, Number 2, June 2018, https://www.journals.uchicago.edu/doi/abs/10.1086/697460?journalCode=jmh.

could hear the screams coming from the men's side of the camp as they were interrogated. In the morning, the women had to wash the bloodstains from the men's clothing. One morning, a woman stopped her washing and said, "This is my husband's underwear."

The setting of the second story is, likewise, in Poland, in 1945, after the end of the war and before Oma and Tante Gretel were "repatriated" to the Soviet Union—to Siberia, that is. The women in the camp were sent out to work in the fields and took their children with them. Oma took her daughter, Gretel, who would have been thirteen at the time, with her.

One day, Gretel was ill, and Oma refused to go out to work in the fields. Other women had lost their children in exactly that way, as the locals would take them. The guards beat Oma to the point of death and threw her on the pile of dead bodies in the camp. That evening, some of the other women saw her stir and went to get her to tend to her. She recovered. Oma Elisabet Franz had kept her youngest child with her, and this child, Tante Gretel, would stay with her and with her future son-in-law, Onkel Adam, provide her with the only grandchildren she would ever know.

The October 24, 2005 eulogy for Oma Amalie Rupp, written by my sisters and I, with an excerpt from Pawlosky, Nadia and Ella Franz, *They say overcoming adversity makes you stronger... Amalie Rupp is living proof*, school project, 2004, reads as follows:

"When the Second World War broke out and the Russians occupied Lemberg, they decided to leave for Germany as refugees. Later that year they moved to Łódź. In August 1944, Oma, Ella, and Lydia were evacuated to Birnbaum (in Poland) while Opa (Hans Rupp) had to stay in Łódź and work (in a Panzerwerkstädte for armoured vehicles). In November 1944, Hardy was born. Opa was able to come for a visit at Christmas to see his family and his newborn son."

My oma, Amalie Rupp, lived in Birnbaum (Międzchód) northwest of Posen (Pozań) with her children, until their flight by horse and open wagon the night of January 17, 1945, in the bitter cold. According to Hardy, his mother, Amalie, was given two hours' notice to flee. She was to pack clothing and three days' food—nothing else. All the gasoline had been requisitioned by the army (the Wehrmacht), but her uncle had horses and a wagon nearby. On their trek, Amalie would cover Hardy's baby carriage with a feather blanket and nurse him underneath it. Hardy's sister, Lydia, remembers that, given the movement of the wagon, Hardy would sleep all day and cry all night. It took three days of travel by horse and wagon to get to Küstrin an der Oder (Kostrzyn), staying in different places at night. The first night, they stayed on an estate. On the second a Polish family took them in for a few days.

In Küstrin, they boarded a train for Frankfurt an der Oder (Frankfurt Oder). Lydia remembers that the train was for mothers and children first and the authorities, taking fifteen-year-old Ella for an adult, prevented her from boarding. Amalie made such a fuss that they ended up pushing Ella onto the train through a window. Otherwise, they would have been separated, as many people were during the flight, never to find each other again.

In Frankfurt Oder, they stayed in a school. They arrived in Leipzig two weeks later, on January 31, 1945, and were given an unheated room on the outskirts of the city. Hardy was very sick and they were reminded that many babies did not survive the journey.

Johann Jakob Rupp had not been able to accompany his family because of his essential work as a mechanic for the Wehrmacht, in Łódź. After the Soviet army landed in Łódź on January 19, 1945, Johann was forced to flee. After several weeks of his trek, Amalie got word through family in Worbis that he was northwest of Berlin, looking for them. The family was reunited. Johann Jakob was then assigned to a Panzerjäger Battalion in Leipzig and worked for them for a few weeks, before being drafted into the Wehrmacht.

Ella started school at the other end of the city (Leipzig) but, after only forty-five minutes of instruction, on April 6, 1945, the bombs started falling on the school. American soldiers entered Leipzig on April 16, 1945, leaving six weeks later, turning it over to the Soviets.

10.

Escape from Leipzig

Johann Jakob Rupp was drafted into the Wehrmacht on April 3, 1945. His Soldbuch shows his rank as "Grenadier" (entry-level) and his trade as "auto mechanic." He was issued a uniform and some equipment on April 4 and then a gas mask on April 5. On April 9, he received a couple of vaccinations. On April 17, he was assigned to a Feldtruppenteil (field troop). There is no record of any weapons issued to him in his Soldbuch.

Recently, my Uncle Hardy relayed this story told to him by his father Johann Jakob. Johann Jakob's unit had been captured by the Americans and the German soldiers were now prisoners of war. Conditions were bad in the American-run POW camp. Johann Jakob said no food or water was provided to the prisoners for five days. Men were drinking out of ditches and dying from dysentery. The administration of the camp was then turned over to the British, and conditions improved. Johann Jakob escaped from the camp and started making his way to Berlin. The only clothes he had on were his Wehrmacht uniform. He pointed to his unit markings on his uniform at every German checkpoint, though the war was officially over by that point, as he was travelling without papers (he needed a letter from his commanding officer to travel legally). When questioned at the checkpoints, he would say he had been ordered to Berlin, where nobody dared want to go. Somewhere along his route, he stopped at an uncle's and had him write out a letter, stating, "this is my nephew, who lives with me in this village."

When he got to Berlin, he said to the German authorities that he wanted to fight the Russians. They replied, go ahead, then! On August 16, 1945, he found civilian clothes and crossed over the German and Soviet lines at night.

He was near the village where his wife, Amalie, now lived with their children, Ella, Lydia, and Hardy. Johann Jakob decided to take a shortcut across a field in daylight when a Russian patrol roared up. They asked for papers, which he didn't have. They asked his business, and he told them he had just finished working at a nearby factory, and was going home to his village. The Russian officer told him they had blown the factory up three days prior and determined, therefore, that he must be a German spy. The officer gave an order to shoot him, and the rest of the patrol raced off. The young soldier left to carry out the order looked at Johann Jakob and said, "You look like you're forty years old. You can't be a spy." He fired his weapon into the ground at his feet and rode away. After that, Johann Jakob decided to travel at night only.

He made his way to the village where he thought he'd find Amalie and the children.

There, though, he discovered they had moved a couple of villages away. So, he made his way there. Amalie had received a telegram from the German authorities that her husband was missing in action. When the neighbours said there was a man delivering coal who wanted to see her, imagine her surprise when she came downstairs to find Johann Jakob, his face all covered in coal dust as part of his ruse!

Though Johann Jakob could have been shot when captured by the Americans, killed by the British for escaping the POW camp, by the Germans (for deserting), or by the Russians, when they had their chance, he was spared at every turn.

At the war's end, May of 1945, the family was in the Russian Zone. American troops had initially taken control of Leipzig after defeating the Germans, before falling back to the line of contact agreed to at Yalta.[67] The Rupps lived in Leipzig until July 1946. Food, however, was very scarce, so they found themselves scrounging for wheat, rye, and potatoes, walking many kilometres in their searches. The Russians were dismantling many factories and sending them to Russia. All the typewriters in Ella's school were shipped off, too, so the students could no longer learn to type.

In July of 1946, the family was able to move to the village of Falkenberg, with the help of relatives. From July 1946 to February 1947, the family lived in

....

67   Wikipedia, s.v. "Line of Contact," last modified on January 28, 2021, at 22:55 (UTC), https://en.wikipedia.org/wiki/Line_of_Contact.

Falkenberg, Kreise Torgauer, Saxony, east of Torgau and northeast of Leipzig. Johann Jakob worked as a labourer for the forestry service and Amalie milked cows, through which they were able to obtain enough bread and milk to regain their strength.

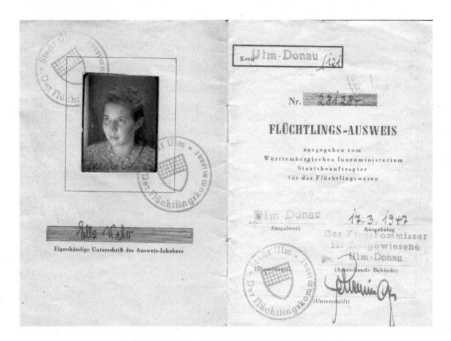

Flüchtlings-Ausweis in Ulm, Ella Weber 1947.

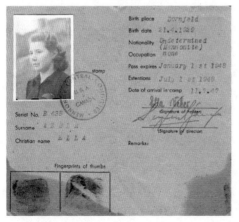

Ella Weber, MCC Backnang refugee camp 1947.

The authorities in the Leipzig area then began to relocate displaced people back to their homelands. The Rupps, who were from Lemberg, Poland (formerly Galicia), were likely to be sent to Siberia if repatriated. Johann Jakob went to see the authorities and produced the letter from his uncle stating he lived in what was to become West Germany. A neighbour of his, a Pole, said,

"This man doesn't live there; he lives in this village here!" Johann Jakob denied this, spoke German only to the authorities, and insisted on his claim, quite bitter for having been betrayed by the neighbour. On the strength of that letter and assistance from the Mennonite Central Committee, who were advocating on behalf of the Mennonite refugees with the authorities, the Rupp family, including Ella, was allowed to leave for West Germany in February 1947.

They were registered as refugees in Ulm, West Germany, on March 17, 1947. They then made their way to the MCC refugee camp in Backnang.[68] In Backnang, there were usually three to four families housed in one room, with blankets used as dividers, which made for a complete lack of privacy. Johann Jakob found work in the tannery, where he was employed from July 15, 1947 to May 21, 1949.[69] Meanwhile, in 1948, the door of escape from the Russian Zone was slammed shut.[70]

....

68   Bender, Harold S., *Backnang (Baden-Württemberg, Germany)*, Global Anabaptist Mennonite
     Encyclopedia Online, 1955, last modified on August 23, 2013, at 13:52, https://gameo.org/index.
     php?title=Backnang_(Baden-W%25C3%25BCrttemberg,_Germany)&oldid=90960.

69   Rupp, Amalie. Eulogy (unpublished). October 24, 2005.

70   Wikipedia, s.v. "Iron Curtain," last modified on February 22, 2021, at 22:00 (UTC), https://
     en.wikipedia.org/wiki/Iron_Curtain.

II.

Refugee Camp in Backnang, West Germany

The Mennonite Central Committee (MCC), the joint relief and service agency of nearly all North American Mennonites, was founded in 1920 by American and Canadian Mennonites, in response to famine in post-revolutionary Ukraine.[71,72] During World War II, Peter J. Dyck was serving for MCC in England.[73] There, he met Elfrieda Klassen, a nurse who had been called separately to serve the organization. After marrying, they were asked to begin an MCC relief program in the Netherlands for Mennonites fleeing Russia, to be followed up by similar enterprises in Germany. Refugee camps were established in several locations, including Gronau and Backnang, where my parents would one day meet.[74]

....

71 Bender, Harold S. and Elmer Neufeld, *Mennonite Central Committee (International)*, Global Anabaptist Mennonite Encyclopedia Online, 1987, last modified on January 16, 2017, at 00:52, https://gameo.org/index. php?title=Mennonite_Central_Committee_(International)&oldid=145869.

72 Epp-Tiessen, Esther, *Mennonite Central Committee Canada*, Global Anabaptist Mennonite Encyclopedia Online, June 2015, last modified on June 20, 2018, at 14:22, https://gameo.org/index. php?title=Mennonite_Central_Committee_Canada&oldid=160924.

73 Thiessen, Bill, *Dyck, Peter J. (1914-2010)*, Global Anabaptist Mennonite Encyclopedia Online, October 2010, last modified on October 6, 2016, at 06:59, https://gameo.org/index. php?title=Dyck,_Peter_J._(1914-2010)&oldid=138826.

74 Dyck, Peter J., *Refugees*, Global Anabaptist Mennonite Encyclopedia Online, 1989, last modified on November 23, 2017, at 07:20, https://gameo.org/index.php?title=Refugees&oldid=155818.

The first 541 Mennonites from Russia and Galicia (Poland) arrived in the Maubacher Höhe and in the Leba (Lederwerke Backnang) in June 1947.[75] MCC gathered the Mennonite refugees from South Germany together, and, very soon thereafter, there were a thousand refugees in the camp, who sought to emigrate to South and North America. Eventually, two thousand Mennonites were able to pass through Backnang to emigrate. By 1950, this emigration came to an end, though, leaving 127 people that were unable to make the move because of political affiliations, their health, or other reasons. Those left behind determined to form a Mennonite Church in 1951 and received assistance from the MCC to build housing quarters.[76]

Johann Franz, MCC Backnang refugee camp 1947.

Backnang train station and MCC refugee camp barracks 1948.

Johann Franz took several photos of Backnang, including a row of barracks that appear to be in the Maubacher Höhe. The Leba, a tannery whose first two floors were taken over as a camp for foreign workers and forced labour, was used

....

75   Lang, Melanie, *Nachkriegszeit, Flucht und Vertreibung der Deutschen*, Backnang im Nationalsozialismus, accessed March 11, 2021, https://www.nationalsozialismus-in-backnang.de/dossier/nachkriegszeit/flucht-vertreibung.

76   "Backnang", MennLex V, accessed March 11, 2021, https://www.mennlex.de/doku.php?id=loc:backnang.

to house Polish displaced persons ("DPs") from April 1945 to February 1946, under American military administration. It was then taken over by the municipal authorities for future housing for displaced Germans. From June 1947 to the fall of 1949, though, it housed Mennonites from Russia and Galicia who were attempting to emigrate.

Johann Franz's bunk in Backnang 1948.

Johann worked as a winder building electric transformers for AEG (Allgemeine Elektricitäts-Gesellschaft AG), which in German means General Electric Company, from January 1948 until May 1949—as a supervisor, toward the end. Meanwhile, the MCC held instructional classes—catechism—for the young people, providing Johann with his first formal religious instruction. He was baptized by Elder Peter J. Dyck on July 4, 1948, upon his confession of faith. This is where it is most likely that Johann met Ella, who had herself been raised in the Lutheran tradition and baptized as an infant.

Johann proposed to Ella on an outing to Thomashof just before New Year's Eve, on December 30, 1948. She accepted his engagement ring and left for Bremen, a city near the North Sea, a week or so later. She was supposed to sail with two of her girlfriends for Canada, but her friends were either denied or had a change of heart. Ella sailed on her own from Cuxhaven on the SS *Scythia*, lifting anchor on January 13, 1949. She landed in Halifax at Pier 21 on January 23, at the age of nineteen.

Ella Weber/Johann Franz engagement 1948.

12.

Coming to Canada:
The Love Letters

Ella had received her visa from the Canadian Immigration Service in London, dated September 27, 1948, which was valid for three months. This visa was revalidated on January 5, 1949 for another three months. Meanwhile, Johann's case had been referred to London for adjudication. The letters (abridged and translated from German by the author) were exchanged between Ella and Johann in the year they were apart. The letters remain in the possession of the family.

Ella's Postcard to Johann on the Alpine Express Train from Stuttgart to Heidelberg.

Undated
Heidelberg

Johann Franz

Backnang

I am really special. I'm not from Poland, I'm from Switzerland![77] Incredible! Greetings, everyone, and don't worry, we will and want to see each other again. Hopefully you can read this because the train wobbles, that's why it's so hard to write. It is quiet now, everyone is deep in their thoughts.

Kisses,

Your Ella.

6.1.49

My dear Hans!

You must excuse my writing this in pencil.... But we hope fate means well with us and that we can see each other in Canada soon....

Kisses,

Your Ella.

7.1.49
Bremen

My dear Hans!

I bought cough syrup and ink so that I could write a proper letter. At home, you can write in pencil, but that doesn't do for the fiancé and dearest one of them all!... Dear Hänschen! If you get notification from London, write me right away by airmail, yes? No matter whether it turns out negative or affirmative! If negative, then we will have to try things differently. We have to have hope, otherwise I would turn around and go to Uruguay with you or

---

77   Ella obviously enjoyed that the train was named the Alpine Express.

stay here just to be with you!! Hänschen, I have such a longing for you, my dear sorcerer, so far from me now. Only my memory of the beautiful hours is left!

But I am very pleased I still came to the train station to see you return to Backnang. It would have been too quick to say goodbye in the camp. I couldn't speak much; my heart was so heavy sitting in the compartment with you. Yes, we all held up bravely. I wanted to tell you all something special, especially Mom, but I couldn't. But when the train left and I stayed alone on the platform, I cried bitterly. I'm not ashamed of my tears. Why should I be, when I left my dearest people?

Kisses,

Your lonely Ella.

Undated
Bremen

Dear Hans!

I would have liked to have sent you an express letter, but it is now forbidden to leave the camp.... There are 27 Mennonites on the list, all families. Hamm, Derksen, Fröse, Dyck, Regier, etc. They leave on the 11th. Perhaps we will leave on the 13th. At any rate, we are not on this list.... You can take 150 kg of luggage per person, including one piece of hand luggage. Our luggage is still in Gronau, in the other camp. Give everyone my love: my parents, first of all, and Erwin, and especially yourself.

From your so-far-away Ella.

10.1.49
Backnang

My dear, dear Ella!

Received your express letter from January 7th today and will answer right away. Perhaps it will reach you in time. Your mom brought your letter to me at work, and I was very happy. I opened it right away and read it.

Dear little one! When you stayed behind in Ludwigsburg and got smaller and smaller and finally disappeared completely in the fog, I wanted to howl out loud! I looked out the window the whole way back to Backnang, so that I wouldn't have to look at your mom.

I received a letter from my aunt in Canada the day before yesterday. They promise to do all that is necessary to get me across. So please don't worry. We will be reunited again. The main thing is that we want to be. If it doesn't work out right away with London (of which I am skeptical), then I will write to all my relatives. And then, it must work out.

Dear Ella! You're a nice girl; I don't think I deserve you sometimes. Hopefully it won't take me long to get over there. What will it be like when I hug you again, after such a long time? Don't make it too difficult for yourself. Everything will be fine.

Now I want to close for today. Hopefully this letter will still reach you and find you in good health and cheer, like a fawn, you little dark-eyed beauty. I wish you a good journey and hope that we see each other again soon.

Kisses,

Your Hans.

11.1.49
Bremen

Dear Hans!

Today I want to write the last lines from Germany. No, sorry, when we board the ship in Cuxhaven, I will throw a card in the mailbox. Then you will know I am no longer on the mainland. Anyway, I am writing my last letter to you. The day after tomorrow, it's onto the ship. I want to face the future bravely and hope for our longed-for reunion! I am eagerly waiting for your first letter!

Warmest regards and kisses,

Your Ella.

Cunard White Star S.S. "Scythia".

14.1.49
On board SS Scythia

My dear Hans!

I would like to thank you most sincerely for your lovely lines. I had lost hope of receiving mail and had resigned myself to my lot. I was overjoyed to hear that I had a letter from you. Tears of sadness and joy fell at the same time. I will be homesick, but I will understand you better, because you have been alone for so long. I now experience it myself. I have not lost my courage, let alone hope.

Best regards and kisses,

Your Ella.

Hann Franz   Backnang, d. 15. Jan. 1949
Backnang, Lager Liba

Sehr geehrter Herr Dyck!

Wende mich heute mit einer großen
Bitte an Sie in einer für mich sehr wichtigen An-
gelegenheit. Da Sie voraussichtlich nicht mehr nach
Backnang kommen, bin ich gezwungen Sie auf
diesem Wege um Rat zu bitten. Es betrifft meine
Auswanderung nach Canada. Bekam gestern eine
Absage aus London, wohin meine Papiere zur
Entscheidung Mitte Oktober vorigen Jahres ge-
schickt wurden. Stehe nun ziemlich ratlos da.
Miss Bawk kann mir auch nicht sagen ob es
noch Zweck hat etwas zu unternehmen. Aber
machen muß ich etwas, habe mich zu Neujahr
verlobt und meine Braut ist im Vertrauen auf
ein baldiges Nachkommen vorausgefahren.
Bin 30% kriegsversehrt. Habe es meinen Verwandten geschrieben, sie versprachen mir alles zu tun

Letter of January 15, 1949 from Johann Franz to MCC's Peter Dyck, page 1.

um mich hinüber zu bringen.

Mir wurde kein Grund angegeben, weshalb man mir absagt. Hatte in meinen Papieren nichts von meinem Dienst erwähnt und das glaube ich ist der Grund, es herrscht Unklarheit über meine Verwundung.

Sollen meine Verwandten nochmal um Einreise ansuchen und alles klarstellen wegen meiner Verwundung und Dienst? Freilich habe auch dann wenig Hoffnung auf Genehmigung, da ich zu lange Soldat war und als Obergefreiter entlassen wurde.

Wäre bereit auch nach Paraguay zu gehen? Aber von dort ist es zu schwer heraus zu kommen, da meine Verwandten wirtschaftlich nicht gut stehen.

Was soll ich machen? Soll ich mich auf das Hierbleiben einrichten? Es liegt ja wenig an dem Schicksal eines Einzelnen. Hauptsache ist, daß schon so Vielen mit Gottes Hilfe gelungen ist eine neue Heimat zu bekommen. Wenn ich hier bleiben muß so will ich es als Gottes Führung ansehen.

Wäre Ihnen sehr dankbar, wenn Sie mir schreiben würden. Möge der liebe Gott Sie auf Ihren Reisen beschützen!

Mit den besten Grüßen und Wünschen verbleibe ich

Ihr Johann Franz

Letter of January 15, 1949 from Johann Franz to MCC's Peter Dyck, page 2.

Johann's letter to MCC (translated from German by the author):

15. Jan. 1949
Johann Franz
Backnang,
Lager Leba

Dear Mr. Dyck,

Today I address a big request to you on a matter that is very important to me. Since you will probably no longer return to Backnang, I am forced to write to you. I'd like to ask for your advice. It concerns my emigration to Canada. I got a rejection yesterday from London, where my papers had been sent for a decision in mid-October of last year. Now I am quite despondent because Miss Brunk can not tell me whether it is useful to do anything. But I have to look for something, I got engaged on New Year's Day and my bride-to-be sailed ahead with the confidence that I would soon follow her. I'm somewhat lamed from my war injuries. I wrote to my relatives, who promise to do everything possible to get me over there.

I was given no reason as to why I was rejected. I hadn't mentioned anything about my military service on my application papers and there may be uncertainty as to how I was wounded.

Should my relatives apply for my entry again and clarify everything about my wounding and service? Of course, even then I have little hope of approval because I served as a soldier for too long and was released as a corporal.

Should I get ready to go to Paraguay in the meantime? However, it is too difficult to get out of there to Canada, because my relatives are not doing well enough economically to assist me.

What should I do? Should I prepare myself to stay here? It doesn't matter much to an individual's fate. The main thing is that so many have already managed to get a new home with God's help. If I have to stay here I want to see God's guidance.

I would be very grateful if you would write to me.

May God protect you on your travels!

With best regards and wishes,

I remain yours,

Johann Franz.

16.1.49
Backnang
(received 7.2)

My dear little Ella!

I want to write my second letter to you today, not sure if you had received the first, in Bremen. I sit here and write while you will be rocking back and forth on the Atlantic between your old home and your new one. Behind you are the memories of your former life and in front of you is the unknown. Do you think of your parents, of me, during these hours? It was a short time we were allowed to be together. Only too quickly came the cruel fate that separated us and keeps chasing us still. We had little time for ourselves and yet I am grateful that I could meet you. You brought light into my darkness after the war years, new hope and new trust . . . . You brought me the love I had to do without for so long. You remind me vividly of my mother, who also loved me very much. Belatedly, I know that today, now, she's not here. I don't know how much I mean to you, but I know that you love me very, very much. If only I could mean as much to you as you do to me! I now have a lot of time to think and reminisce. Everyday a memory of you comes to mind, but you are no longer here, and I am as lonely as before.

Yesterday, I was in town. We were still working in the morning, the second Saturday now. I walked through the streets of Backnang, looked into the shop windows that I so often looked at with you. But I don't see you in the reflection— I'm alone! Then I go on, walking for hours, until it starts to rain, and as it gets dark, it grows so dark inside me, too, because you are no longer here. I go home and have the long evening ahead of me. I imagine you are in the next room, but you are no longer here. You are alone somewhere, on the sea, hurrying, on the ship, toward an unknown future. I shouldn't have let you go, but what can I do about it now? You have obligations towards your loved ones, too. They have to go over to safety first; only then can we think of ourselves.

Everyone has their mistakes, and I have a lot of them. I think you know me very little. You are a lovely little creature and deserve a lot of love and happiness. God grant me that I can give you both. Dear Ella, I also pray for you, may God protect you on all your paths so that nothing bad happens to you. I've enclosed two photos of our engagement. Do you still wear the ring? Hope this letter gives you a little joy when you arrive over there, to have something from me in your hand.

And now I say goodbye, warmly and with many kisses,

Your Hans.

21.1.49
On board SS Scythia

My dear Hans!

Soon, we will be in Halifax, and I would like to write you a few lines. Thank God I'm fine now, rid of the bad seasickness. Dear sorcerer! Do you know what I'm doing?! I've been keeping a small diary since I left Bremen. Perhaps, if you are quite good, you will get to read it once. But only maybe! I can tell from your lines that you find it awkward to go to my parents. Why? They love you and, as their future son-in-law, you are welcome. Now I will conclude, in the hope that my letter will find you in the best of health.

Kisses,

Your Ella.

29.1.49
Russell, Ontario

My dear Hans!

Now, it is not as we wanted it to be. Unfortunately, I didn't go to Kingston, as I wrote to Mom. It's a shame, but my boss promised me that when it gets warmer, *he will drive me to Kingston by truck. So the reunion is postponed. I will write to Aunt Otti today so that she will send me your mail, because I am eagerly waiting for it. I've been gone a month. Much can happen in that time. Maybe you already have your visa and are on your way. Anyway, if that is the case, send me a telegram from the port, so that I know. And then, please try to go through Ottawa on the way to Saskatchewan. There are two routes to Saskatchewan: one via Quebec and the second via Montreal and Ottawa. And from there you can call me. Ask for "Russell No. 54 Tel." One train comes here. You will receive $10 upon arrival in Halifax. Hopefully, that lasts you till you arrive here and then we will see what we can do from there. Sorry to write about this first, but it seems to me more important than anything else.*

Now I want to satisfy your curiosity and write to you, dear Hans, about how I have made out. I look after two children, a four-year-old girl and a boy (with blue eyes!), who's one and a half. They are nice kids, and so fat! The people are very friendly, but I'm only here the second day. Above all, they are very happy to have someone here. The other men and women I've met so far are very nice and friendly. My employers, my lady and gentleman (ordinary people), have a lunchroom next to the kitchen. It is open all day, except Sunday, until 2 or 3 a.m. (as I was told today). However, it is not my job to work in the lunchroom, they do it themselves. I am a domestic servant and, so far, I have helped with serving dishes and doing a lot of dishwashing. However, most of the work is early in the week, so I haven't much to say about it yet. If I don't like it here, I will go to Ottawa and find a place. I could have stayed there, but I said yes to Russell (because Kingston was not possible). Maybe it'll be easier for my parents to do something here. After all, that's why I came to Canada.

I believe I've worn out your letter, reading and rereading it as it's been so long since I've heard anything. You all have it better in this regard, since I've been so diligent in my writing! But you will now compensate me for it and write to me often, won't you, my beloved Hänschen?! Your Ella is waiting impatiently for this! You write that the many new impressions I'm encountering might dull my memories of the past. Oh, no. My thoughts are always with you and my dear ones. Now I will close, because tomorrow is a hard day.

Kisses from your Ella. Say hello to anyone who asks about me!

1.2.49
Backnang
(received 14.2)

My dear Ella, my little baby!

I couldn't wait until I received a message from you and so I wanted to write to you again. I received your letter from the ship; you cannot imagine how happy I was to receive news from you so quickly. How are you, did you survive the trip well? How did you find it? What are your impressions of Canada? You will hardly be able to get an idea of it so quickly, but you have sharp eyes. I have a lot of questions, but I don't want to fill out the whole sheet. You know what interests me: what you're doing, how you're doing—in a word, everything, everything!

Of course, you also want to know how I am and what I am doing and so I want to write to you briefly about what I have done during this time that you've been away from me. It's not going well for me. I miss you so and think a lot about you. I also have a lot of time in the morning when I go to work, during the day at work (which is mostly mechanical), and in the evening before going to bed. I am so full of longing for you, my dear little one. You are far, far away from here. The Atlantic lies between us and so I am only with you in my thoughts, every day.

You know, I will probably have to stay in Germany longer than we thought. On January 13th, the day you went to sea, Mrs. Rupp came in the evening and told me go see Miss Brunk the next day. You can imagine how I felt the day you left. I had such a dark feeling, then. I thought it would be the same old story about immigrating for me. At noon on the 14th, I went upstairs, and she told me my immigration application had been refused in London. And now, dear Ella, I have to beg your pardon for not writing it to you straight away, but I was so depressed those days that I could have only written you a very sad letter. And I didn't want you to receive such a disturbing message when you arrived over there. Please don't be angry with me for that reason. Today, I can write to you with more courage. It's a heavy blow, but it's not the first in my life, and it shouldn't get me down this time, either. I'll just have to start all over again. I immediately wrote to Peter Dyck, who had gone to Switzerland, but still have no answer.

I want to write to my relatives and to Mr. Thiessen from the board in Saskatoon, where my relatives have made application for me.[78,79] *I was not told a reason why I was rejected, but assume that it is because I was wounded and said nothing about the Wehrmacht. I don't want to rush this time and will go through everything correctly. It has to work! For you, dear Ella, this will also be a heavy blow, but please don't be discouraged. We have a good Heavenly Father who holds our story in His hands and guides us. If it is His will, and we also want to come together, it will be. Of course, it will be a big test for both of us, but I think if what we both think what we felt was real and that we deserve each other, we will get back together. America is not Siberia, and there will definitely be ways and means for me to get across.*

I want to close for today.

With many regards and a thousand kisses,

Your lonely and forlorn Hans.

P.S. Be a darling, dear girl, keep your head up! It may look so black sometimes, but the clouds have to disappear. The sun wins every morning!

5.2.49
Backnang
(received 10.2)

My dear girl!

Received your precious letter, that I had been waiting for, this afternoon. Now, I know where you are and want to write you. Today is Saturday. It will

78   Patkau, Esther, *Thiessen, Jacob Johann "J. J." (1893-1977)*, Global Anabaptist Mennonite Encyclopedia Online, July 201, last modified on February 12, 2014, at 05:21, https://gameo.org/index.php?title=Thiessen,_Jacob_Johann_%22J._J.%22_(1893-1977)&oldid=112831. J.J. Thiessen was chairperson of the Canadian Mennonite Board of Colonization, on the executive board of MCC, and in 1948 visited refugee camps in Europe, seeking to open doors to bring displaced persons to Canada.

79   Gerbrandt, Jacob, *Canadian Mennonite Board of Colonization*, Global Anabaptist Mennonite Encyclopedia Online, September 2011, last modified on February 24, 2021, at 11:25, https://gameo.org/index.php?title=Canadian_mennonite_board_of_colonization&oldid=167400.

be mailed today and in 4-8 days it will be with you, far away. My dear little one, you are all alone now. We were certain that you would go to Kingston, like the others. Now, you are on your own, and I can only visit you with my letters, which I want to do often. You should get something from me every week. It will also be very difficult for you, as you love socializing, but I think you will make it, you brave little one. Do you know that everyone here in the camp is amazed that you had the courage to go alone into the wide world? And I'm happy because you are like that. If it is sometimes difficult for you, think that we are with you, and that I believe in you.

You know, here, the memory of you lives in me, here, we got to know each other. All the ways that I go during the day I have already walked with you. I often think about what lies behind us and wonder whether it was right how I behaved. I'm not always sure, but we have to leave that to the future and to God. So much still lies ahead of us, but we don't want to let it get us down. If you only will wait for me!

Best regards and a thousand kisses,

Your Hans.

If only I could soon take you into my arms and hug you tightly! You dear little witch, you!

8.2.49
Russell

My dear, dear Hans!

Tonight, before supper, I received your dear and heartfelt letter, which Aunt Otti forwarded to me. I had been waiting for it. Thank you very much for your lovely lines. My heart was full, but I didn't know what to write then.

Be well, dearest.

Kisses,

Your Ella.

Swing Cams .　　　　　　　　　　　*FRANZ*

Gronau/Westf., den 4.2.1949
PJD./O.

Herrn
Johann ~~Franz~~
~~B a c k n a n g~~
~~Lager Leba~~

Sehr geehrter Herr Franz.

Ihren Brief vom 15.1.49 habe ich erhalten. Ich gebe Ihnen volles
Verstaendnis fuer Ihre fast aussichtslose Lage. Sie sind scheinbar
dafuer dankbar, dass mit Gottes MCC-Hilfe recht viele, bereits fast
1o.ooo nach Uebersee gelangen durften. Doch schreiben Sie auch, dass
wenig an dem Schicksal des einzelnen liegt. Ob ich daraus schliessen
soll, dass Sie mutlos geworden sind weiss ich nicht. Jedenfalls
teile ich in diesem einen Fall Ihre Ansicht durchaus nicht, denn
ich glaube bestimmt, dass gerade das Schicksal des einzelnen in
den Vordergrund treten muss und wir werden dass Fluechtlingsproblem
nur dann loesen, wenn wir bestaendig mit jedem einzelnen Fluecht-
lingsleben rechnen. Letztenendes ist dieses auch der Weg Gottes.
Er rechnet nie mit der Masse, sondern immer nur und ausschliesslich
mit der einzelnen Person.

Was Ihrer Auswanderung anbetrifft, so glaube ich nicht, dass eine
neue Herausrufung von Canada helfen wuerde,. Wenn Sie, wie Sie
schreiben, 30% kriegsversehrt sind und als Obergefreiter entlassen
wurden, liegen die Dinge nicht gut.Dass Sie fuer Sued-Amerika
wenig Interesse haben, kann ich gut verstehen.Wir wissen auch nicht,
ob und wann wieder ein Transport gehen wird. Sollten Sie anderer
Meinung sein, jedoch muss ich darauf hinweisen, dass wir grundsaetz-
lich nur solche mitnehmen, die Sued-Amerika als Endziel und nicht
als Sprungbrett betrachten. Mit einer kleinen Gruppe junger Maenner
haben wir mal eine Ausnahme gemacht, doch sind sie alle noch
in Paraguay und wir wissen noch nicht, was mit ihnen werden wird.
Jedenfalls war das von unserer Seit einmalig und eine Ausnahme, die wir
hoechstwahrscheinlich nicht wieder gestatten werden.

Ich bin nicht einer der bald dunkel sieht und zum hierbleiben ratet,
aber so wie die Dinge bei Ihnen liegen, muss ich es Ihnen auf-
richtig sagen, sehe ich in absehbarer Zeit keine Chance zur
Auswanderung. Ich kann es verstehen, dass es Ihr sehnlichster Wunsch
ist Ihrer Braut zu folgen und ueberhaupt ein neues Leben anzu-
fangen. Doch sind die Aussichten hierfuer sehr gering.

Es tut mir leid Ihnen keinen guenstigeren Bescheid geben zu koennen
und gruesse Sie als
　　　　　　　　　　　Ihr

Letter of February 4, 1949 from MCC's Peter Dyck to Johann Franz

MCC's letter to Johann (translated from German by the author):

Gronau/Westf.,
4. February 1949
PJD./O.

Mr. Johann Franz
Backnang
Lager Leba

Dear Mr. Franz.

I received your letter dated 1/15/49. I sympathize with your almost hopeless situation. You are probably grateful that, through MCC with God's help, quite a few, almost 10,000, have been able to go overseas. You write that the fate of the individual doesn't matter as much. I do not know whether I should conclude that you have become discouraged. In any case, I do not share your view in this one case, because I certainly believe that the fate of the individual must come to the foreground and we will only solve the refugee problem if we constantly consider every single refugee life. Ultimately, this is also God's way. He never reckons with the crowd, but always and only with the individual person.

As for your emigration, I don't think that a new call from Canada would help. If, as you write, you are somewhat lamed from your war injuries and were discharged as a corporal, your situation does not look promising. I can understand that you have little interest in South America. We also don't know if and when transportation will be up and running again. I have to point out, however, that we only take people with us who regard South America as their ultimate destination and not as a springboard. We made an exception with a small group of young men, but they're all still in Paraguay and we don't yet know what will happen to them. In any case, this was unique on our part, and an exception that we will most likely not allow again.

I am not one who loses hope easily, but as things are with you, I have to tell you sincerely, I do not see any chance of emigration in the foreseeable future. I can understand that it is your most dear wish to follow your bride-to-be and start a new life. But the prospects for this are very slim.

I am sorry I cannot give a more optimistic opinion.

Regards,

Peter Dyck

11.2.49
Backnang
(received 21.2)

My dear, dear Ella!

You made me very happy with your dear letter from the ship and I have to say that I liked it a lot, because it contains something of your dear nature. Do you know, dear little one, that my thoughts are with you all day? In the morning, when I wake up, the first ones belong to you and, in the evening, the last ones. I often wonder at work what my Ella is doing right now.

You must have already received my letters and know how it is with me. I now have a hard time with this uncertainty, and my letters will be so messed up afterwards. I can't write what I want to write to you. Got an answer from Peter Dyck. He thinks my prospects are also not very favourable. It's not all lost yet, but I'm afraid it will take a long time, and every day without you seems eternal to me. You know, if you weren't over there, I would just as soon forget the whole thing. But this means waiting, hoping, working. And, by now, you may have forgotten me, or it may take too long, and you might change your mind. You are free if you change your mind. You are so alone there, and I am here. You already know me a little. You know more about me than everyone else. You are the only one I love. I often think I'm not worthy of you. At least, I know there is no other girl in the world like you. Do you remember how I told you I wish for few friends, but real ones? Well, I count you the very best!

It is nice of you to keep a diary. I will be very happy to read it, but I have to be good, so I will try very hard. I also had diaries. The first one I had was in

Russia, but I destroyed it, because there were things in there that could harm me when the war came. As a soldier, I had another one, but it was lost when I was wounded. It would be nice to start again, now, but it takes time, which is in short supply. I will write to you, my dear. This should be my diary, but I fear, now, that everything is going haywire, crisscrossed, like my thoughts.

So, goodnight, dearest!

14.2.49
Russell

My dear, dear Jonny!

You say that I really know very little about you. You do know me much, much better than I know you, that's true. But that's not so bad. I do know something of you, and believe everything you tell me and assume, when you failed to tell me something, that you must have had your reasons or else that we didn't have the time.

It will be difficult for you to start in Canada, because you will have language difficulties, at first. But that's only in the beginning. I think when my year is over, I won't have any more problems. It's no wonder if you only speak English all day! I am concerned about how it will be for my parents. When we want and are allowed to get together, the beginning will not be easy, but it will be easier than in Germany! A new start is always difficult.

Please say hello to everyone I know. And you, yourself, have all my hellos and kisses.

Your Ella.

P.S. It's a sad birthday, this time. For this, I paint my lips and press a kiss on the forget-me-not card, but it's only for this purpose that I adorn myself! Hope to spend your birthday, next year, with you.

Lots of kisses from your Ella, so far away. Write to me very soon!

19.2.49
Backnang
(received 26.2)

My dear Ella!

I received your dear letter of February 8th and, today, I want to answer. I have been waiting for this letter very keenly, since you could write a little more, now, then at first. You had been in Canada too little time, in your new location, to get a good perspective. What you actually mean to me has only become clear now that you are no longer here. I have already dreamed of you, once. Oh, that it weren't a dream, but a reality!

When you wrote to me that you would have stayed here if I had said something, I realized what a mistake I had made. But I was firmly convinced that my situation would work out and that I would come soon. Had I known how it would turn out, I wouldn't have let you go. But you never know what the right thing to do is.

Of course, I have to confess to you, when the news came from London, I was very depressed, and was already considering Paraguay. But what would I do there? I would have to wait there, too, and it is very uncertain whether I could ever leave, so I soon dropped the thought. I know God will guide us and, if it is His will, and we want it too, when we are strong enough to pass all tests, we will be reunited.

Now, I want to tell you something about our camp life. I'm sure you'll be interested. Prof. Unruh[80] was here today, and tomorrow, he will hold Sunday service. I like him very much. He has something manly about him, and a firm trust in God. I wish I could be like him.[81] We should have more men like him

---

80   Bender, Harold S, *Unruh, Benjamin Heinrich (1881-1959)*, Global Anabaptist Mennonite Encyclopedia Online, 1959, last modified on February 24, 2021, at 22:58, https://gameo.org/index.php?title=Unruh,_Benjamin_Heinrich_(1881-1959)&oldid=132460.

81   Jantzen, Mark and John D. Thiesen, ed., *European Mennonites and the Holocaust*, (Toronto: University of Toronto Press), 2021. B.H. Unruh served the interests of his Russian Mennonite brethren in emigration and resettlement as commissioner for the Canadian Mennonite Board of Colonization for the immigration to Canada in the years 1921-25 and later for the MCC in immigration to Paraguay 1930-33. He is a controversial figure because of his ties to the National Socialist Party, the Nazi Party.

and Peter Dyck, or Mr. Klassen.[82] *It would be better for us. In Russia, the best men were taken from us and sent to Siberia—ten rather than one, a hundred rather than ten, so there was no man left who could lead, and pose any threat to the government.*

I also asked our work counsellor as to whether it would be possible for me to obtain a profession (or trade) at AEG. He thinks I will be ready in 1 to 1½ years and told me to consider electro-mechanics. What do you think about that? Should I grab onto it, if I get the chance? I mean, if I can come over, I will come over. But I don't want to sit around idly for a year or two; it is high time to get established, as I am now 24 years old.

I dreamt of my mom last night and saw her in a courtroom where she and other women were sentenced to 10 years in Siberia. Saw the guards clearly with their bayonets. When my mother was taken away, I had to cry. Unbeknownst to the authorities, I was also in the courtroom as a spectator. I was sentenced to death in my absence. I cried, and then I woke up. My father's birthday was on February 13th, and he would be 60, if he is still alive. A few days ago, I also dreamed of my sister. I received a letter from Schleswig-Holstein. She was there without our mother. Maybe they really are separated somewhere in the world. I can only be with them in my dreams. I dream very often, lately.

For today, I will close. Goodnight, dear girl, goodnight. "I'm just a poor journeyman," you know.

....

82   Bender, Harold S. and Richard D. Thiessen, *Klassen, Cornelius Franz "C. F." (1894-1954)*, Global Anabaptist Mennonite Encyclopedia Online, May 2013, last modified on June 12, 2020, at 05:08, https://gameo.org/index.php?title=Klassen,_Cornelius_Franz_%22C._F.%22_(1894-1954)&oldid=168316. C.F. Klassen was the European Commissioner for Refugee Aid and Resettlement Aid under the MCC in Europe from December 1945 to his death in 1954. He handled the negotiations with various governmental and international agencies including the UNO and IRO for exit permits, transportation, and migration for over 10,000 Russian and several thousand other Mennonite refugees to Canada, Paraguay, and Uruguay.

19.2.49

Dear Ella!

I found a dictionary here. Hopefully, it will serve you. There are no pronunciations, but you will not have any problems with it, and, if you do not know something, you can ask. And one more thing, dear Ella: if you need anything, please write, because, after all, I am your fiancé. If I can find it, you should have it.

Greetings from your parents and siblings. I also greet you warmly and kiss you many times.

Your Hans.

20.2.49.

Dear Ella!

Just want to end this weekend's letter to you as Sunday winds to a close. Tonight, Prof. Unruh gave a very interesting lecture on Mennonite emigration from 1923-1929. It took a long time, from 7-9, but you could listen to him all night, without getting tired. His motto is: "He (God) can help". I also want to take on this saying, for myself. You know, I wrote the following words in my war diary: "When clouds pile up in the dark and stormy black waves rage, think of your distant home, and you will not be alone". When I wrote this, I had another home in mind, which does not exist anymore. But this still remains valid. I have found a new home, which nothing can take away from me. I often think, these days, that, even if I am denied the visa and passport for Canada, I have already received another passport that no government in the world can take away from me: namely the certainty that God will help us if we look and surrender to Him.

I have also received the news from my relatives that they looked into the immigration process and there is still no information about the rejection. Things move very slowly. I spoke to Miss Brunk today, too. Unfortunately, the time was short, so I have to talk to her again. She thinks it would be possible for you to sponsor me, but that is out of the question, since you know me little, and probably would not take the risk, since you would have to marry me in 3 months. Did you receive the certificate of engagement?

For today, this should suffice. All my thoughts and desires are yours. May the Lord protect you and keep you until we see each other again.

Kisses,

Your Hans.

Undated
Backnang

Dear Ella:

I want to finish my letter. It's late again, but people are still up, the children still awake. There was a bit of snow last night. I photographed it today to complete a roll of film. Tomorrow, I will send it off, but I'm afraid there isn't much on it, as when I took it out, some of the film got exposed to light. I'll see. It costs to learn.

You also ask what a pogrom is or whether I know about it. I have not experienced it. In the past, the Jews were robbed in Russia and their stores smashed. The same happened after 1933 in Germany.

Enough for today. I hope to get news from you again, in the next few days. Until then, my warmest regards and kisses are with you.

Your lonely Hans.

P.S. Received your lovely letter from 14.2. today. I will have to answer it next time. I am glad that you feel as I do.

And now, with warmth and kisses,

Your Jonny!

21.2.49
Russell

Dear Hans!

You actually don't deserve a letter from me! No mail from you for 2 weeks! You bad person, you! When you know how alone I am here, waiting for mail. Or do you have a lot to do? I think of that as an excuse. If it's not true, then I'll make you wait just as long! This time, you're lucky to get a letter.

It was a good thing that I replied when I did, as your letter about the rejection from London arrived. Only on Thursday, when I had time, did the meaning become clear to me. It was a bad day for me, but now it's over. You just have to deal with things as they are. How about the girls? Will they leave you alone? I have my anger here. I have told people here many times that I don't want to have a boyfriend, but they don't believe I'm engaged. I can find it hard to believe too, we are engaged and yet so far apart? Do you find it difficult to believe too? But don't let your courage sink! Head up, dear Hans! I was asked by the boys working here whether I would dance and I said "No", and then they offered to teach me (there are 2 boys of 23 years working here). I only want to dance again when my parents and you are safe, and then, to be dancing with you! I haven't been to the cinema or to see a hockey match yet. I have no desire to. The main topics of conversation here are sports and the weather.

With warmth and kisses,

Your Ella, waiting for mail.

24.2.49
Russell

My dear Hans!

Today is Sunday again, and so, I would like to start a letter to you. I wrote to you on Friday, but in a hurry. Do you know how long you will linger in Backnang? I ask the dear Father in Heaven that you will soon be in Gronau, and then, on your way here.

You take fabulous pictures. When are you going to snap your bride-to-be? I dream that you could take such colour pictures with your camera, but that it will be too expensive for us. And you, with the family. You, you, you!

You know, Hänschen, you are my Hans, not Jonny. Only, when I sing the song, "My Bonny is over the ocean," then I sing, "my Jonny" is over the ocean!

24.2.49
Russell

My dear, dear Hans!

Today is your birthday, and my thoughts are mostly with you. I am very happy that you now have such a beautiful camera. How much did it cost? Dear Hans, are you sending me some pictures of yourself, also? Since I can't be there, I would like to see how my Hans looks. Do you understand? I would still like to be with you, whether it is going well or poorly.

What you actually mean to me has only become clear now that we are apart. But I can't put it into words. Do you understand me? I actually have to apologize a lot for my last letter. Now I am not so sad. I am confident again. I was so homesick. Now, I'm waiting more patiently for your precious letters! My dear poet! Did you also write something about your Ella? If not, then definitely in your heart! Is it true, dear? Thank you very much for your valuable letters, as I get to know you better through them.

Heartfelt regards and kisses,

Your Ella.

P.S. Yesterday was a difficult day, but today it was cozy. Kisses from Ella.

27.2.49
Backnang

My dear girl!

Now, I want to answer your dear letter from 14.2. First of all, thank you very much for your birthday greetings. I was very happy about the card. When I saw your lips on it, it was like kissing them. The memory is still very vivid to me. You bad girl, who didn't want to kiss at all!

Your letter also made me very happy. But, dear Ella, you always think of others first. Sponsoring me wouldn't be that quick; I don't yet know how we should do it. It might be better if you sponsored me, but you have to think about it very carefully. I would be ready at any time, but I am sometimes afraid of the material situation; we are poor, like two church mice. And you also know that, with my wounds, I am not quite up to par.

Ella, I wrote to you in the last letter that I made a mistake, certainly, if I can't come over. You remember, last year, when we danced together for the first time? How short the year was. Far too short. You write you are glad that you did not leave in October. We would not have gotten to know each other as we now have. We both would have known far less about each other, far too little for what we are going to do. But sometimes, it weighs on my conscience; if we don't get together, I will have a heavy load to bear for letting you go. But we have to reunite. I don't lose heart, but, sometimes, I have difficult hours. I know you feel the same way, even though you don't write it. I think I can read it between the lines. Now, let's be patient and wait, which is difficult for me.

Many kisses,

Your faraway Hans.

6.3.49
Russell

My dear Hans!

I would like to thank you, in particular, for your lovely letter, which I received last night. You know, I'm a bad girl. I didn't write much to you the last two times and wrote my parents more. Actually, I prefer to read letters and dream than to write. I find it, as you do, much harder to put everything in the written word, as opposed to when I speak, I think.

You bad, bad Hans! Do you think I'm not worried about the material conditions?! It would of course be more advantageous if you could get over here. But in Germany, things would be somewhat taken care of, as you were injured in the war. You would be able to speak German at work. I don't know how it is with work here. You cannot speak the language here. It will be a difficult start; you have to be prepared for that. I believe that our love is strong enough to overcome all difficulties. I don't think another man will ever mean as much to me as you. How did you, sorcerer, manage that? Cheer up, Jonny!

And how are you, my old grandpa, with your learning in English? Aren't you too old for that? Have you already started with electro-mechanics? You might be interested to know that, here, "115-120 volts" is written on the lightbulbs. I will also ask my employers about it and then I will write to you.

And now I close, with many warm regards and kisses,

Your Ella.

9.3.49
Backnang
(received 15.3)

My dear Ella!

I have been waiting on a few lines from you every day. Now, I can't take it any longer, and want to write to you. You have spoiled me with your diligent writing. What's wrong? Did you take my advice to heart and decide to write with ordinary letters (not with airmail)? Or is it something else? Maybe I wrote something that you don't like, or that you took a little differently than the way in which I meant it? Or did I make a mistake? Dear girl, just don't be angry, and forgive me, if that is the case.

How terrible it is that we are so far apart. I want to speak to you, I want to kiss you, I want to take you in my arms and hug you. But that is no longer possible. Dearest, do you still think of me, or have you already completely forgotten your Hans? You probably think he has also forgotten you. It is not so!

Now guarantees have arrived for 1000 families to be sponsored to Canada. Your parents have also applied. If it works out, you will at least have them over there. What will happen with us is still to be determined. You know, dearest, if, for the time being, I don't see any way of getting to you, I still have the firm confidence that everything will be fine. Now I kiss you warmly again, my dear sweet little girl. Don't forget your Hans, even if he wasn't always what he wanted to be or should be. We are only human, but we can try to be better.

A thousand times a thousand kisses,

Your lonely Hans.

15.3.49
Backnang
(received 22.3)

My dear Ella!

Yesterday I received your dear letter from February 21, for which I had to wait so long, and which made me very sad for its brevity. Do you have nothing to say to your Hans if a letter from him takes longer to arrive or are you slowly forgetting me? Now I want to answer you, maybe a letter will come from you again tomorrow, maybe not. But please don't think it's just you that waits for a reply. I wrote to you regularly; 10 days was the greatest interval from one letter to another.

You ask me if the girls leave me alone. Which ones do you mean, the ones in the camp, or others? Do you really know your Hans so poorly? Do you think I'm a womanizer? I was not in the past and certainly not now. Why did I get engaged, then? Just write to me if you want to wait for me, just write if you still love me or else that, after such a short time, you think I might not be the right one.

I think of you often. Please don't forget me completely. And even if everything was in vain and I have been wrong, I will be glad to have met you. We spent many nice hours together and I will never forget you.

My dear, little, precious Ella, be kissed by your Hans, who looks at you from afar, and is very, very sad when he has no mail from you.

16.3.49
Russell

My dear Hans!

I received your impatient letter with the same impatience. In the meantime, you will have probably received my letter from February 22, which has the same tone. You know, dearest, your letters are precious to me and, when things are difficult for me, I gain new courage and strength by reading your dear lines. You know, I have to concentrate a lot during the day; by evening, my nerves are so tired that I don't feel like writing anymore. So there is a lot of unanswered mail now, but I write to you every week. I had taken your advice to heart and wrote with ordinary mail, but I had put $2 in the February 22 letter. Maybe it was lost. That's why I'm writing today by airmail (you see, I'm not so stingy!), although I've already sent two letters in the meantime. I think I'll write by airmail again because it otherwise takes so long. I was somewhat depressed in the previous letters; but now things are going better. I have had to learn a lot, especially self-control, have had to laugh (though I've felt like crying), and have had to practice a lot of patience looking after my employers' children. I've never been in a position like this before, as a domestic servant. I am now dependent on others.

I kiss your dear, dear picture every time I come into my room, dearest! How could I forget you?! You are the first one that I love.

Love,

Your distant Ella.

20.3.49
Russell

My dearest Hans!

I'm reading your dear, precious letter from March 9. My thoughts wander to you, so I would like to put some on paper. I have locked you in my heart, my mind and thoughts belong to you. My love for you has never changed. We always want to be open to one another. Trust!

I am glad you have found a purpose through youth work and I am always very happy when you write about it. It's a shame I can't be with you now; hear what my fiancé is saying! Goodnight for today, love, sleep well!

Today, Tuesday, came your dear letter from March 15th, which also made me very sad. If I only had known the letters take 3 weeks to get there! And this one, too. During this time I have become more patient, more trusting, and stronger. I am, of course, waiting for your letters, and the nicest reward of the day is a letter from my beloved Hans! I know you are not a womanizer; I didn't mean it that way. I know you in this regard. And how can you doubt your Ella? I have only revealed my heart to you.

A thousand kisses,

Your loving Ella.

21.3.49
Backnang
(received 25.3)

My dear, dear Ella!

Although I have no mail from you since your last, very short letter, I want to write you a few lines again. I read all your dear letters again tonight and agree you were much more diligent in writing than I, but I want to do as much as possible to catch up. I have your first postcard from the train, and your dear letters from Bremen. This period, your last days in Germany, were the hardest for you. Then, there are those from the ship, in which you are already composed. Your gaze is directed more toward the future, but you also think back on your loved ones in Backnang. In front of me is the picture of the ship, the ship that kidnapped my dearest and which I sometimes would rather have never been built. Then, in your first letters from Russell, in the rush of first impressions, my dear little Ella shows her practical side.

What are you doing now? Do you still think of your Hans, or have you already forgotten me? The next letter for which I am very impatiently waiting will give me an answer to some questions. I am happy about your last letter but, at the same time, it also makes me sad, because it shows me how lonely you are. Your homesickness is even clearer in the letter to your parents. I am homesick too, but it is not focused as in your case on a certain place. I do not know whether any of my loved ones still live, and I have no home. It was destroyed, and everything was taken away from me. Do I have anyone on earth who cares about me? I think you do, but I'm not always sure of that, either. Well, nothing's there to save us; everyone has to carry their burdens with them, some more than others. Write to me very soon. I have such a longing for you, little, darling, sweet girl, you could never know.

Many hugs and kisses,

Your Hans.

27.3.49
Backnang
(received 1.4)

My dear little Ella, my dear bride-to-be!

Now, I have two lovely letters from you to reply to: the one from February 24 and the one from March 19, for which I thank you very much. I have been waiting for your letters very eagerly, expecting them to answer my questions, which they did. Thank you very much for your kind words. I see you haven't forgotten me. I have to tell you honestly that I didn't completely believe that to be the case. How can you always be so certain? I ask that you please don't hold it against me.

I was with your parents again tonight and talked to your mom about you. You are more like her than you think. Otherwise, she would not be so dear to me. I think your parents also like me. Hopefully it will work out for them with Canada soon, although, if I get left behind, I will be doubly alone. Otherwise, I'm fine, if not for the terrible loneliness and uncertainty. But we are all in God's hands and, if we deserve it, we will reunite.

All my kisses and love,

Your Hans.

30.3.49
Russell

My dearest Hans!

I received your dear letter from March 21 at the same time as my parents' letter. Thank you very much. I was very happy to receive your lovely pictures. We could be together again soon and snap photos together; wouldn't that be nice? Hope for the best. Has Mr. Klassen returned to Backnang? If you want me to sponsor you out, I'm ready. The Kingstoners want to try to get me there, but now I've settled in, and I don't really want to move. Time flies so fast; tomorrow, it will have been 9 weeks that I've been here.

I am waiting for you, because I love you and, therefore, I am not interested in other men. I'm cool, as always; still friendly, but quite reserved. Please don't lose hope of seeing each other again. You can trust me in everything, as I do you, dearest.

A thousand kisses from far away,

Your Ella.

3.4.49
Backnang
(received 8.4)

My dear little one, my dear Ella!

Now it is Sunday and I want to write you again. First of all, I apologize for my letter. It was not meant as you may have taken it. You know me. I always want to earn your trust. I fully trust you.

Mr. Klassen was here last week, telling us about the emigration. He told us that the camps here are to be closed. Those who were in the SS and the Wehrmacht should first look for something here, he told us, the others should go to Gronau.[83] Once most of them are gone, they will take care of those whose applications have been put on hold for health reasons, except those with TB or trachoma. They then want to engage the government again. Yesterday, I got a letter from my cousin, who told me he had gotten a letter saying I had been rejected for health reasons. If that is the case, I still have a chance. Of course, I might have it easier here with work, but how can I be without you? My heart belongs to you alone. And I will also find work there. I want to ask my relatives to guarantee my sponsorship with the government; it has to work then. I don't think you can do anything for me on your own. I pray every night: If it is your will, Lord, please let me get back to my Ella. Now, for tonight, goodnight.

A thousand kisses and hugs,

Your Hans.

....

83   Bender, Harold S., *Gronau Mennonite Church (Gronau, Nordrhein-Westfalen, Germany)*,
      Global Anabaptist Mennonite Encyclopedia Online, 1956, last modified on January 16, 2017, at
      00:28, https://gameo.org/index.php?title=Gronau_Mennonite_Church_(Gronau,_Nordrhein-
      Westfalen,_Germany). In 1946-1953, Gronau was the seat of the extensive refugee aid program of
      MCC. Gronau served as a transit camp and springboard to Canada, Paraguay, and Uruguay.

7.4.49
Backnang
(received 13.4)

My dear girl, my dear birthday child!

First of all, I wholeheartedly wish you all the best and God's blessings on your 20th birthday! May God bring us together by your twenty-first! I want nothing more. My thoughts are always yours, but on April 21ˢᵗ, they will especially be with my dear, dear Ella! And they will fly back to the time when you, little one, were here in Limburg. You know when I was still very shy and I still hesitated to give you anything, for fear you might reject me. I could not imagine you would one day be my Ella, my little dear sorceress. Look at all that's happened in this one year! And how quickly it flew by. It was like a beautiful dream. But, unfortunately, it seems much too short to be real. Do you think, Ella, that Spring will come for us, too?

Goodnight, you sweet little girl, with a thousand kisses and hugs; though only in the thoughts of your Hans.

8.4.49

My most beloved fiancé!

Got your letter from March 27 and, today, the letter from April 3. I received it happily. Thank you very much. Especially for the violets, very kind of you. Got a very nice letter from your aunt. She wrote to me that she thought what you have to carry is almost too much: your dear home is lost and now, we are separated. She wrote that I should stay loyal to you, even if it may take a while until you come. She prays that we can stay true to each other and reminds me of how nice it will be to see each other again. I agree. It was very kindly written by your aunt.

Kisses,

Your faithful Ella.

15.4.49

Dear Hans!

My hope has not been disappointed: I received a very nice letter from you. I will answer soon, after my birthday, because I will probably celebrate in Kingston. My people won't be driving me, so I will take the bus for about $5, and can stay longer. For how long I don't yet know! I'm so looking forward to it! Dearest Hans! You didn't say anything about a gift for me? Why? But Mom mentioned it.

Warm regards and kisses,

Your Ella.

15.4.49
Backnang
(received 21.4)

My dear girl!

I want to start a letter to you today, but I will probably not finish it, because it will probably be a long one again. Please don't be upset. You know I sometimes forget and then regret it later. I haven't received anything from you this week but, tomorrow, I hope to receive a little letter from my dear, little fiancé again.

On Friday, Mr. Peter Dyck and Siegfried Janzen[84] came to Backnang. We had to fill out questionnaires because the camp is to be closed. There were quite a few questions, 99 in total. Then we had to present it in person; I came before S. Janzen. Then I told him about my case and gave him your address. My case will be brought forward again, on the list for 2000 immigrants in

84   Penner, Peter, *Janzen, Siegfried (1920-2005)*, Global Anabaptist Mennonite Encyclopedia Online, 2006, last modified on January 5, 2021, at 00:02, https://gameo.org/index.php?title=Janzen,_ Siegfried_(1920-2005)&oldid=147018. Siegfried Janzen volunteered for MCC service after completing his alternative service in Canada during World War Two. He and his wife Margaret worked with the General Relief section in Holland at first, distributing food and clothing to refugees. They were switched to the Mennonite Aid section in 1947 where they helped develop a camp at Gronau on the Holland/German border. Over a three year period he directed the processing of more than 10,000 Mennonite refugees at Gronau.

the British zone. But since they are to be guaranteed sponsorships of families, I asked if it would be possible to join your parents (they have also listed me and Erwin too on their questionnaires). If it works (if), I will come together with them. Only, I ask you to be patient, and not too optimistic, as you know what difficulties exist with emigration. Even if you already have the visa, it can take a few months (as it did with you). In any case, the 2000 immigrants are to be resettled by November.

Only, I fear that if Gronau doesn't work out for me, I want to go back (to Backnang), because of the work. This still has to be negotiated with the AEG management there to see if they would take me back. It would be fatal if I travelled back, but found that I had lost my job, and then wouldn't have funds to get away. Now, it is time to save again, so that I can have money for an emergency. I have bought different things: a hat, briefcase, shirt, pants, and so on. I want to buy a good suit, oh, I want this and that, but it doesn't always go as you want, or as fast as you want. Now, the main thing is that we stay healthy, and the other things will come.

I spoke to Peter Dyck very briefly. He is now leaving the MCC for home. He lives in Saskatoon, and I asked him to send greetings to my relatives. He told me, "We'll see each other over there."

You, little girl, are still shy. We got engaged, but we didn't have time to talk about getting married. I understand your impatience completely; I feel the same way. If I come with your parents, we may be settled close to you. We'll see. But don't be impatient. We don't know when and how it will happen. But it's a step closer.

And now, with many warm regards and kisses,

Your thoughtful Hans.

Undated

Russell

My darling!

I would like to write to you again, but will not finish the letter, because something may come from you soon, right? Today, I received the letter with the birthday greetings from my parents. A nice gift is coming from my dear, too; I am looking forward to it already and am excited to see what it is. Thank you, in advance, most sincerely!

Someone offered to drive me to Kingston, on his motorcycle, if I became his girlfriend. But, as always, I try to think of others before myself. I want to look my Hans openly in the eye! If your conscience is clear, it is worth more than anything else, dearest!

Above all, I'm looking forward to the days in Kingston, and I ask God for good weather. Dearest, you need not be afraid. I am, I believe, in no danger of falling into a trap. Maybe I'm worried about you.

Well, for today, goodnight, my best comrade!

19.4.49

Kingston

Dear Hans!

I arrived here yesterday. I was so tired that the first thing I did was have a good rest. We made the most of our time together, although for me it went much too quickly. Still it was very nice, I got to see how things are here. Now I'm not sure what I will do. If I relocate here from Russell, I would probably get paid more and also be with my friends.

In my thoughts, I kiss you many times!

Your Ella.

24.4.49
Backnang
(received 30.4)

My dearest Ella!

Today is Sunday again, and it was my turn to reply to your letter from April 15, with great pleasure. I would be happy if you were able to go to Kingston. Hopefully it worked out, and you weren't disappointed, and spent a few nice days there.

You're actually a bad girl. You only write when you're missing something, when it's already over. Do you always wear the ring I gave you? Whenever I see mine, I think of you, and recall what brought us together. You don't have a picture for the locket yet, but you still carry me in your heart, don't you?

Now, I want to close for today, because it is late.

A thousand kisses,

Your longing Hans.

1.5.49
Backnang
(received 6.5)

My dear Ella!

Now your beloved lines from Kingston are in front of me, and I am happy that you had a wonderful Easter. I would like to believe that you probably didn't sleep much, and I don't want to know what you talked about—Oy vey, you women! Yesterday, I was in the sawmill, and ordered boards for a crate. Slowly, I have to get ready to travel.

Today we have another wedding in the camp. They didn't know each other for very long and only got engaged two weeks ago. Sometimes I regret letting you go, but you're still a little young, and it's good to get to know each other beforehand. I wouldn't mind, though. We could get married right away. Because

I'm pretty lonely and still young enough—but also old enough—so why should I wait?

You know, we have a very nice little boy here, now, in the room, and I'm sometimes jealous because he is not mine. The little guy laughs all day. Hardi also likes him very much. Hardi is looking pretty good, now.

No longer work on the winding machine. I have now become a supervisor and have to take care of 4 machines, for the time being. Next week, we are supposed to start working the night shift, because we have a rather large order, and too few machines. Perhaps there is also a prospect of a wage increase. We all want to give up 50% of our pay this month, without exception—anyone who has any income, including the workers in camp—since the MCC needs 5,000 marks for the hospital. And so, my suit will have to wait, for the time being. If I can travel with the 2000, I will at least have no travel debt to pay, because the costs will be covered.

I can hear the accordion and noise from below. And your Hans is very lonely. When I hear the accordion like that, old memories awaken in me. I have to think of one evening in Russia. We had just set up our field hospital and the first of those who had been seriously wounded arrived from the front. It was the spring offensive of '42. Inside, people were dying, while, outside, there was music. Life goes on!

It has now gotten much better in Germany, and a German government is also expected to come soon. I have calmed down a bit now. We have to wait and hope we can be together again.

Goodnight, my dear girl, dream of me.

With many kisses, I remain yours,

Hans.

8.5.49
Russell

My darling!

I received your dear letter with much joy and gratitude. Dear Hans! Thank you for being so honest with me. I don't want to cheat on you, either. Why did you change your job? Running around is definitely going to be difficult for you. But you have a firm will and what you decide to do, you can do. Just like the dancing, right? It's a shame you can't buy a suit, but it will come. Do you have to give 50% of your wages every month?

Here, too, there's a wedding almost every week. The boys get married very young. With us, we will have to wait and see how it works out for you and my parents. For the time being, we don't have to make any decisions, right? But I don't regret that I went to Canada. This time is very instructional for me and, in Backnang, I was still too much of a child, and really not ready for marriage. Marriage is a script for life and it demands a complete person. Time brings a lot with it and I'm more serious, now, including in my feelings for you. That's why the men here do not interest me. When we reunite, it will be so much nicer! I understand your loneliness; I'm lonely here, too. But your letters are a joy for me, and I read them again and again. But life goes on. I, too, came to this conclusion, and that's why I want to carry on as intended. How will I receive you? With open arms? Just come, too!

Warm regards and kisses,

Your Ella, dreaming of you.

8.5.49
Backnang
(received 17.5)

My dear Ella!

You know, I was a little sad last Saturday when the mail came and there was nothing from you. But I'm not angry with you because of that. Maybe you didn't get to it, or it was delayed a bit. You know, I've gotten used to receiving

95

something from you every week. Please don't make me wait too long, because I'm very lonely. It is no longer nice in Backnang; the camp has already emptied out. And I myself am in two places—I am here, but my heart is in Canada. We live in complete uncertainty, but we live. Eventually, though, you want a resolution. But there is nothing you can do, just wait and hope. If hope wasn't there . . .

And what are you doing, dear girl? How is work going and what's on your mind right now? Are you still thinking of changing jobs? In Kingston you would have more variety. What would be better is difficult to say from here. I hope you will get it right.

Today, on Tuesday the 10ᵗʰ, I will continue to write. Yesterday, your dear letter (from April 24th to May 1st) arrived. Please excuse the beginning of my letter; if I had known you were sick, I wouldn't have written like that. As I wrote you in the last letter, I am now working shifts, a week from 2 p.m. to 12 midnight and this week from 6:30 a.m. to 2 p.m. It is an adjustment and it is somewhat difficult to eat regular meals with the shift work. I am responsible for 5 machines and their operators now. It is not very easy for the girls to work because the machines do not perform as they should. When I worked on my own, it was easier. Time does go faster now, though, because I have to walk around a lot. The AEG has now grown quite large.

With many kisses, and thoughts of holding you tightly,

Your loyal Hans, who longs for you, you little sorceress, and often thinks of you.

12.5.49
Russell

My dear Hans!

Today is my Thursday again and I want to use the evening to respond in more depth to your most recent, dear letters and, also, to report some things to you. My work is not dictated to me and that pleases me. I have given up the thought of changing positions. My employers are really nice, I may eat what I want, I have every Sunday free and, today, my employer said she will pay me $40! I will now mop the restaurant floors on Wednesdays, too, so that my employers can rest. I don't have any special work, just keeping things clean, helping with meals, dishes, and the children, and helping with the guests. But we're not very busy here. It is, after all, a village.

Will I please you now? I cut my hair off Tuesday night! Do not be alarmed, but it is so. My employer helped me. It's pretty short now, but that's definitely good for my hair. I enclose a lock of my hair for you. I kept one too, because in this hairstyle I got to know and love you and how often your hands ran over it! But when you come over my hair will have grown longer!

Regards and kisses,

Your lonely Ella.

15.5.49
Backnang
(received 21.5)

My dear Ella!

This is probably the last time I will write from Backnang. Next week, Wednesday or Thursday, we will go to Gronau, another step closer to our goal. It came as a bit of a surprise for me; I had expected a later date. It's always like this. You wait and wait and, in the end, it seems to come too fast. I leave no one behind, just my work, so it is not so difficult for me to say goodbye. It may still take some time, but I sincerely hope and pray that emigrating will come soon. Hopefully I don't have to wait too long in Gronau without work, because it is very unlikely that I can return here. I talked to our engineer and he told me he can't guarantee 100% that they'll take me back. I will talk to the director again tomorrow. Of course, I would prefer if I didn't have to come back, and don't think I will have to, either. Now that I am halfway familiar with my new work, I had to say yesterday that I was going away.

70 people are travelling this week. Hardi is really looking forward to it. But he wants to take the baby with him, he says. I suggested we could take the baby

if we be very quiet when people are sleeping! He likes that very much. He has now gotten a pair of Lederhosen, which he is very proud of.

Leaving is not difficult for me, probably unlike it was for you. In Gronau, Erwin[85] and I only want to learn English. And whatever else we must do will be shown to us. Gronau is now full, because the 2,000 are all gathered there. Then, the Commission will get there. I used to really want to travel. During the war, I wanted to be somewhere else every day. It's a shame that I didn't have a camera at the time. But today, I'm not into it so much anymore. This Saturday, our young people wanted to travel from the factory to the Black Forest, but now, nothing will come of this. I have not seen much of Germany. But sometimes I think I might still see a lot of the world. That everything I once dreamed of as a boy might come true. Who knows where our paths will lead? It's a shame that we couldn't sail together. I would have gotten a lot more out of the journey. But maybe we will in Canada, or somewhere else, if you do want to travel with me. Do you want to, my dear, little girl? Or are you not for traveling?

Warm greetings,

Your longing Hans.

MCC D.P. Camp in Gronau ID Johann Franz 1949.　　The "barn" in Gronau 1949.

....

85　　Erwin Andres was the nephew of Johann Jakob Rupp.

22.5.49
Gronau
(received 28.5)

My dear Ella!

Today, I want to write you, for the first time, from Gronau. I arrived here safely on Thursday, after a 14-hour journey. It is not too big, here. Inside, there are compartments made with blankets, double beds, boards to stand on, and little light—only from above does it sometimes penetrate. Very cramped—there are 9 people in our room. Erwin and I are together. I have to go back to the IRO, having already filled out questionnaires, and given everything truthfully.[86] Was also in front of Siegfried Janzen. The IRO is due to come this week. More Backnangers came again yesterday. Most of them are already here, and some of them have to lie on the floor today. We have some unsettling weeks ahead of us again, but I am now very calm. It will not be as bad as in Ludwigsburg. I have a clear conscience and the belief that everything will be fine, despite everything. We won't be here as long as we've been in the camp so far. Either way, this situation of abnormal camp life cannot last. I'm glad, at least, that you already have this behind you, and, even if it isn't everything there that you expected it would be, things will be OK. We'll reunite, so long as we want to. And we do want that, don't we, my dear, little one?

I have an aunt here, in Gronau; she lives 2 minutes away, in private accommodations. She's all alone here. One of her sons was a soldier and is missing, probably in Russia. I was in a class with him. The other son, a 20-year-old, is also in Siberia. Her daughter is married in Belgium and wants to emigrate to Canada from there. My aunt does, too, from here. So now, we're all scattered around the world. Your parents were so reluctant to come here. Your father said several times that, if you were still here, he would not emigrate. It was like they suspected something. Here at the Schützenhof, a traffic road lies nearby and, when we were here one day, it happened. Hardi was hit by a motorcycle and is now in hospital with a very serious injury. Your parents now have a

....

86   Wikipedia, s.v. "International Refugee Organization," last modified on December 1, 2020, at 17:35 (UTC), https://en.wikipedia.org/wiki/International_Refugee_Organization. The International Refugee Organization was an intergovernmental organization founded to deal with the massive refugee problem created by World War Two.

very difficult time ahead of them. They are always taking turns being with him. It has affected your father a lot. Today, I visited the hospital. Hardi asked for me and recognized me immediately. He is very cheerful and brave. The nurses like him because he is so calm. It hurts me as if he's my own brother. When you get this letter, you have to be brave. It is in God's hands. It is very difficult for me to write this. I was also wondering whether it is right to write to you about it now, but I have to, and it is better to do so right away. Hardi has a head injury. Please be brave, dear Ella. He is in God's hands, and I pray for him.

Warmly, with kisses,

Your Hans.

22.5.49
Russell

My darling!

Thank you for your lovely lines, which always delight me. I give you a warm kiss for the pretty pictures. Hardi looks really nice, especially now, in his Seppel pants, don't you think? What have you done with the baby? Did you manage to take him with you at night?

I am wondering if you have made it to Gronau and how you have arranged it with the AEG. It would be much nicer if you didn't have to go back. I will pray and ask God to let all of you, "Family Rupp," come over. When I read your card about travelling to Gronau, my heart was pounding. Hopefully, it's a step closer! In the Mennonitische Rundschau, I also read about the people in the Backnang camp being relocated.[87] 184 applications for 633 refugees were confirmed, but they're still asking for additional applications. As I see it, Peter Dyck has it under control.

87 Bender, Harold S. and Richard D. Thiessen, Mennonitische Rundschau, Die (Periodical), Global Anabaptist Mennonite Encyclopedia Online, June 2007, last modified on October 31, 2019, at 17:36, https://gameo.org/index.php?title=Mennonitische_Rundschau,_Die_(Periodical)&oldid=165973. The Rundschau was the paper of the Russian Mennonites for decades and was published as a German language periodical in the U.S. and Canada.

I firmly believe it will be fine. The commission is not supposed to be so strict. You may have trouble getting though with the wound, but don't fail, please. It would also be nice if you are able to come to Ontario, it would be good Toronto - Hamilton. But how do you know what's good? Now, I want to write you something about my work. A lot has changed. I now have more tasks, which is my own doing. I have promised that I will serve, from time to time, in the restaurant. And also bake (this baking is not an art!). It already has some advantages. I am learning to serve, my English is getting better, and it is good to do what you can. As a result, I have sweets and more than $40 in wages in the summer months. And I especially enjoy the learning. Since I also have to do the housework, I can't take on too much work like this, though.

Please, write to me now, often, even if it is hard for me to hear about your health. And keep me up to date about the emigration! Should you and Erwin go to British Columbia? So far from here? To Western Canada! 4-4500 km! That's as far as from Halifax to London across the North Atlantic! The distance worries me. Oh, it hurts me so much to hear of Hardi. How could this happen? Once you get these lines, you may already know more. I am always with you in my thoughts. I pray to God to bring us together! I am so sad. I will finish this letter to you, and then write to Mom.

Your Ella.

28.5.49
Gronau
(received 3.6)

Dear Ella!

I have settled in a bit, moved to a room with a lot of young people, and already have a camp bed, so things are better now. It is noisier, but you get used to it, over time. I passed the IRO too, I've made a start now, told everything truthfully and so I was pretty calm. Erwin also passed the IRO.

You know, your last letter was also a bit surprising. Why did you actually have your hair cut off? There is a danger that I may suddenly realize that I no longer like the way you look. I would like to see how you look now. You haven't thought of that? What do you think of that? Do you no longer care what I might think?

Kisses,

Your Hans.

3.6.49

Dear Hans!

These little things are for you. Had prepared it for a long time and today I want to send them to you. Please don't be angry with me for getting my hair cut, OK?

Regards,

Your Ella.

4.6.49
Russell

Dear Hans!

Yesterday, your 2ⁿᵈ letter came from Gronau and, at the same time, the news that Hardi is doing better. I am very pleased. I was so worried about him. The crisis is not over, but with God's help, he will get well. How nice that your heart is so attached to him. Here, the little boy is such a nice kid. I love him. He laughs a lot. The little girl is quite stubborn, so I do not want to have to sleep with her. It may be that I will swap locations.

I gather that you don't like me helping in the restaurant. I do more here than at the ones in Kingston, and the earnings are worse. I don't mind the work much, but why should I overwork? Nevertheless, the other work has to be done, too. Children come a lot to the restaurant. If only that were little Hardi or Lydi! But this time may come, too.

Your Ella.

5.6.49
Gronau
(received 13.6)

My dear Ella!

I have been neglecting you recently; please excuse me. It has been very stormy for me lately. So please do not be angry with what I wrote to you about cutting your hair off, though I would easily deserve it. I would like to know why you did it. Have you already become so English?

I have settled in a bit here, but it is going bad, especially because I have no work. It is difficult to wait. Especially when you see what you can buy here. It will probably take us a little longer, because of the accident with Hardi. But thank God he's fine. He's a brave little guy. I didn't think he would bear the pain so patiently, because he's otherwise pretty impatient. If this had not happened, we would also be like Erwin and the Rudolph Rupps[88], in the first group, for which the medical examination will start tomorrow. The first group is due to travel in mid-July, the second in September. If everything goes well, we'll be in the second one. Well, we'll see. Just be patient and hope and pray. We can't do anything beyond this. Waiting will be as difficult for you as it is for us, but, on the whole, I am calm. Certainly, if you were still here, I would not let you travel there alone, because I have long since realized what you mean to me, much more than when we were together. I would like to look for work, if only I can find something here.

Your Hans.

....

88   Rudolph Rupp was a relative of Johann Jakob Rupp.

11.6.49
Russell

My dear Hans!

You want to know if I'm still angry with you, because of what you wrote when I cut my hair off. Of course, I'm not giving up hope that I'll still please you. You know, actually I haven't changed anything else, my hair is just shorter. Please, forgive me, if you can!!! You are probably being selfish, though, but it is always good if we express our opinions to each other, if only in writing.

I had some friction with my boss on Sunday evening. I had a debate with her a little earlier. You know, I spoiled them. I worked really hard, and on my own initiative, from 7 am to 9 pm, mostly without a break. Once, I went to the living room at 7 pm, after washing the dishes (since my room was being wallpapered), as I wanted half an hour for myself, until half past seven, when the children go to bed. And, on Monday, the fuss started. Immediately after breakfast, she gave me the bill for my 8 days away in Kingston and 2 days off for illness and wanted to dock my pay. Then, I said I wanted to go to Ottawa to change jobs—to switch to Kingston or Ottawa. I wrote straight to Kingston, but I haven't had any mail from there since I visited. What's going on there? As you can see from these lines, there's been a big commotion, these days. But I did it. I got my full salary, my room to myself again, and shorter working hours. They don't want me to leave, but they take advantage of my situation. But since, on July 12th, they want to go to New York for 2 weeks, I want to endure. Then, I will be my own master.

Goodnight, love!

13.6.49
Russell

Today your dear letter came, for which I thank you from the bottom of my heart, and which I received with joy. I get on well with you and I think we will understand each other even better now. It is so beautiful that you want to give me your heart completely. It is enough for me. I also want to give you mine. During this time, it's become clear to me that life is a struggle. But we hope that, if God wants it, you can make it here in September. You know, it's been so hot the last few days. But better than rain, yes. It's raining work, though! I've had a lot to do; but it's been fun. But because she, my employer, complains and doesn't pay more, I will put an end to it. Keep learning English, please!

Your Ella.

20.6.49
Gronau
(received 25.6)

My dear little Ella!

Another week has passed without anything special happening to us. Time has been dragging for me and I didn't want to write to you. They come from time to time: the blues. This waiting is difficult to endure. It happens, the moments when you doubt God and people. And if you then think back to which camps you were already in, and recognize there was always a way out, you can look to the future, and trust God.

It's all right. If your employer, your lady, is so hysterical, I wouldn't want to be there for the long run, because that's something I can't take. I would get in a row every day. If the others didn't last longer than 1-2 months, you have been there long enough. But you have to know for yourself; it is difficult to judge from here. Just don't worry about your hair. I can't see it now and if I come over you can wear it the way we both like it, right?

The Canadian Commission is here today, and the first have already passed through. It is not clear what will happen—one former Wehrmacht soldier is accepted, and another is not. We will see how it goes. Erwin is through. If nothing comes in between, he will soon be over there. It seems that it's best not to tell the truth, because most pass through. I can easily imagine how it will be with me. But the main thing is that your parents get through with this push. I will then find a way myself. I don't have high hopes this time. The young men may now want to try to find a way to England instead, but I will wait and see. That's the way it is with us. But I don't want to give up, just clench my teeth together and keep fighting. Just believe in me and our luck, then we

105

will reunite. In spite of everything, there must be justice in the world and, if we deserve it, we will get back together. Just don't lose faith, even if sometimes, it looks like lying will help.

Your mom will definitely want to write something. Right now, she is in the hospital visiting Hardi (who is fine).

With many warm regards,

Your Hans.

23.6.49
Russell

My darling!

I know I want to change positions. It is possible to go to Ottawa more easily than to Kingston. But my people don't want to let me go. That's why I have decided to act and rid myself of Russell in this way. Because I haven't had it easy. When does Erwin leave? Have you decided to wait until my parents depart? You are already part of our family, are you not? It's actually good if you come together; then you'll arrive in the same place. Hopefully, not in British Columbia. Yes, I also feel this tension, as you do, and I pray to God I'll see you again soon. I trust in God's guidance. Then, when you're over here, it's up to us. Will we still understand each other, then? Soon, we'll have been apart for as long as we knew each other in person!

Kisses, dearest,

Your Ella.

30.6.49
Gronau
(received 6.7)

My dear Ella!

I received your lovely letter from June 23, for which I thank you very much. I can see you have a lot of grief with your employers and difficulties in making the change. But why is it so hard to get to Kingston? I think it would be nice to get to know Ottawa, but I'm afraid you'll be pretty alone there, too. In Kingston, you could at least get together with the others on days off. Will you be able to get out of there?

Now it has become a bit quieter again, the commissions are done with their work. Some can immigrate, others have failed. That's just the way it is. I am happy if someone can immigrate, even if I can't yet, because the hour will come for me, too. You ask why I didn't come alone. My application was linked with your parents. When Hardi got in the accident, the work commission had just been here. I didn't consider coming alone and, later, the commission was gone. Now, your dad says I should come alone, if they can't. I also tell them that if they can't immigrate because of me, they should just come alone, because it is questionable whether I can get through. It takes a lot of patience to wait so long, especially when you are out of work. I went to see the farmer this week, looking for work, but there was none. Here in Gronau itself, there is little work. You have to surrender 50% of your earnings, and then live like this. But lying around is also difficult. I attend English lessons but can't say I'm making big progress. I lack the necessary calm and diligence for study. I've never been lazy like this in my whole life. I rarely get up before 9 a.m. Nothing is going on in Gronau, either. You can walk up and down the few streets, but that soon grows old.

You know, it is doubtful we would have gotten so close without being sepa-rated. I want to see it as fate, for my part. I am thankful I met a girl like you, and that we understand each other. How else would I have known what you meant to me? And would we have become engaged if you hadn't been leaving so quickly? But now, you have my word, and I can calmly wait in trust for you. Why are you afraid that I might go to B.C.? If I come over this autumn,

107

I definitely want to earn funds for my journey. I want to arrive close to you, if I can, but I think I may have to go further away. What do you think? What are your plans when your year is over?

Was at your parents' just now, but nobody is at home. They probably went to see Hardi. He comes out of the hospital on Monday. Since there is still time until the commission, I hope he will continue to recover.

With many kisses, I remain yours,

Hans.

30.6.49
Ottawa

My dearest!

So, now I have landed in Ottawa, but not until Monday, July 4th will I decide whether I go on to Kingston or stay here. If I find a good job here, I would like to stay. Sad that you are not here. But this time will come, so please do not give up hope.

I had a bad dream today. We were all still in Germany. The Russians were supposed to come. You tried to jump over the canal to England. With one foot, you reached the shore, but you fell into the water again. My heart was pounding, and I was with you, Hans. How are you? Healthy and at the Commission? I feel very comfortable myself and am happy to finally be gone from Russell. I liked the waitress job, but I didn't like seeing the mess in the restaurant every morning, even on Sundays. In the evenings, I would leave the kitchen in perfect order. In the mornings, I would have to tidy up the restaurant, clean up the food and waste on the tables and on the floor. Then, breakfast. The children! They were very clingy and the little one called out, "Ella!" often. I was fed up.

Kisses, from one country to another,

Your dark-eyed Ella.

2.7.49
Ottawa

My dear Hänschen!

This is my 2nd letter from Ottawa and, this time, I can write you a lot more, and more calmly. I mostly have been spending the days with the Martin family. I will certainly help out, because there are things to do. I feel very at home in this family group. They are not Mennonites; they belong to the "Brethren".[89] *When my year is over, I will probably want to do something else. There are more factories in Toronto. That may be possible, later. I have my own bathroom here, which I am very pleased about. Here, I can also learn French. I will soon have my new job! I received $45, and will receive more, later, when the grown children come home. He is a General (English) and the mother is French. What do you have to say about that? Irma Stauffer wrote me that they want to leave Kingston, so I thought it might be better here. I have found friends in the Martin family here and, through them, friends in the church.*[90]

With warmest regards,

Your Ella.

6.7.49
Gronau

My dearest Ella!

Got your dear letter from June 30th today. Actually, yesterday. I want to write right away so you don't have to wait that long. Today, I worked as a switchboard operator in the MCC telephone exchange. It is just a few minutes after midnight and therefore the telephone exchange is no longer in operation. Now I want to take the opportunity, because there is a heavenly calm here and I can really chat with my girl.

....

89   Wikipedia, s.v. "Brethren in Christ Church," last modified on February 8, 2021, at 14:20 (UTC), https://en.wikipedia.org/wiki/Brethren_in_Christ_Church.

90   It is not known if Ella stayed in contact with the Martins. It is likely that the Martins were connected with the work of MCC.

Hopefully, you will be better off in the new position. You poor little girl. You had to work pretty hard. I can imagine the company very well. And if people are not nice to you, it is much more difficult. I am glad you keep your spirits up and are brave. This has probably been a very hard lesson for you, my dear little one, and I can only be proud of you. Hopefully, I'll be over before your year is up, and so will your parents.

Now, I want to tell you some things from here. First, something very gratifying. Your little brother came home yesterday and he's just as lively as before. Of course, he remains your parents' problem child. Above all, your father suffered a lot from this accident. But thank God everything's gone well so far.

Hopefully I can get through the commission. The processing of the second group has now started. However, the first group is not yet gone. Even if you stay in Ottawa, I fully trust you. You know, we got to know each other so slowly last year. I don't remember the actual date, back then, by the moonlight. I only know it was wonderful! It's been just half a year since we last saw each other, but what an eternity it's been. An eternity full of hopes and disappointments. But I have courage again. Not always, but on the whole, I do. If it doesn't turn out this time, either, let's try again. It has to succeed eventually.

How do you like it in Canada? Don't you feel homesick for Germany sometimes? English is unlikely to be a problem for you anymore. I hope to learn it, too, especially if you'll help me.

Your far, faraway Hans, in Gronau.

13.7.49
Ottawa

Dearest Hans!

Thank you very much for your lovely lines from July 6th. The letter only took 5 days. Now, you have received my last letter and know that I stayed in Ottawa. I am satisfied with my work. Russell was a good lesson for me and we need one for life, too, because life doesn't always teach you with kid gloves. Here, I have everything in perfect order. I have my own bathroom (well, I also live in

Rockcliffe, the richest neighbourhood). The kitchen so pretty. It is a pleasure to work here. Don't I have it good? Of course there is work, still, but why did I come to Canada if not to work? I get paid. My boss was a General of the Canadian Army in Europe and comes from a family of officers.[91] I'm not homesick anymore. Canada is a beautiful country. Only I am longing for all my loved ones.

Actually, it is very strange that you've been such a loafer lately. Do you want to do that in Canada, too? Then you don't belong in this country. Because here, they are short of workers, and you have to master all kinds of work. Can you and do you want that? What a question! That you want to make pancakes for me is splendid. What do you like, fruit or jam? The men in Canada mostly know more about cooking than the women do. The General, too. I said I can't cook at all. But I get to eat hearty food. There was no such thing in Russell.

Your Ella.

13.7.49
Gronau
(received 18.7)

My dear Ella!

Now I have your dear letter, in which you wrote to me that you will remain in Ottawa. Thank you very much! I am glad that you have met such good people, who help you. When you go to the Martins' again, please greet them and thank them on my behalf. I think you did it right. Hopefully you are lucky with the new job.

Had phone duty again yesterday. Do duty every night. Your father is now also employed. He is now an intermediary between the MCC and the second group. He has to make sure that people are always informed in good time about the processing. The processing has now started, and I already have been to the

91   Hall of Valour - Temple Du Courage, *Ralph Holley Keefler*, accessed on February 27, 2021, http://www.canadaveteranshallofvalour.com/KeeflerRH.htm. Major-General Ralph Holley Keefler (1902-1983) was the general officer placed in command of the 3rd Canadian Division in 1945.

X-ray. *The labour commission is due to come next week. Keep your fingers crossed. I myself don't count on it very much. It would be a miracle.*

Hardi is fine. He jumps around again, as if nothing happened. I didn't think his recovery would be this fast. You see what prayers can do. Hardi also prayed. He is a nice guy. He came to visit me a few days ago. I wasn't there, just then, so he went home and said he wouldn't go to Uncle Hans's anymore, because I wasn't at home. Otherwise, we get along well. He really likes me. Yes, your parents are now accommodated in the big hall. Maybe not for long, if they get through OK.

I remain yours,

Hans.

20.7.49
Ottawa

My dear Hans!

Received your lovely letter on the 18th, for which I thank you. This time, the mail went very quickly. I see there's some news. The 1st group is on the way and the 2nd has started processing. I can well imagine your feelings; I feel that I also deal with these questions a lot. I think, after such a long time of waiting, that you don't feel like emigrating anymore. Then all of a sudden it works. So it was with me! But I hope it will work anyway!

Ella with her short hair!!! Don't be scared of the way I look!

Your faraway Ella.

Ella in Ottawa 1949.

22.7.49
Gronau
(received 29.7)

My dear Ella!

I received your dear letter from July 13th. I am glad to hear you are finding
things well in your new position. Hopefully, it will stay that way. I said to your
mom, hopefully Ella will continue to write to us, now that she's with a General.
But you don't seem to be in danger, at least not yet, perhaps later? But, if you
no longer write, you will, of course, not hear from us anymore.

Of course, you are curious about how we are doing. Well, not much has happened this past week. The Labour Commission was supposed to come but didn't.
Now I've seen the junior doctors. So far, everything seems to be OK. When
it came down to it, I did not mention my war wounds and the doctor did
not see the lameness either, although he did see a scar. I was a little riled up
when being examined and therefore my blood pressure was a little too high for
comfort. I want to hope for the best, but I'm preparing for the worst. You feel
bad when you have to wait like this and wait again, but it is now time to give
up as in 2 weeks I know more. What I will do if I fail I don't know yet, then I
have to start again somewhere. You don't want to deal with this thought at all,
but it keeps coming back. But it's really no use. Comes the time, comes advice.

Your Hans.

24.7.49
Gronau
(received 2.8)

My dear Ellalein!

Yesterday, I received your dear letter from July 20th. Many thanks for the
pictures! I was already curious how you look now, and now I can look at my
Ella again. Were you afraid of what I might think of your hair? It's not bad,
it looks good. And your hair is still long enough for me to mess it up! When
you sent me your lock of hair, I got a real fright. I see, now, that my fear was in

vain. Beyond that, I think you've gotten thin. And with your hat, you look a bit American, but otherwise better and nicer.

Lots of kisses,

Hans.

25.7.49
Ottawa

My dear Hans!

Since there is still a lot I did not get to say in my last letter, I want to write to you about it now, though there is no dear letter from you in front of me. I hope there will be something from you soon. On Sunday I was with the Martin family in Rockcliffe Park and we had a picnic with ice cream. Then, we drove to their home and I went to church with Mrs. Martin. I learn better English through the word of God and the songs. People are also very friendly. Am I not doing fine? It's fabulous. Delicious food, just like at home. Chicken every week and everything with cream, I can't describe it to you. My new employers want me to start cooking, but I only plan to stay for 6 months and therefore have been reluctant. By the way, yesterday, I made 2 pancakes from one egg. Tasted wonderful. I think you would have liked them too! You write about cinema. 1. I am not interested, and 2. Why should I spend the money? What I wanted to write to you about the Martins and the "Brethren", they don't dress up and don't go to dance or cinema. They take Holy Communion every Sunday morning. I feel comfortable and at home with these people. They don't drink alcohol and most don't smoke. It's good that you don't smoke, so we can save our money for something else.

I dreamt of you tonight, love! I don't quite know what actually motivated me to cut my hair. Probably because it is quite warm here and I am feeling confident. My hair also grows very quickly and is much thicker. How do you like me in the pictures? Am I the old Ella or not? If you get through, be thankful to the Lord, and if you fail, which I hope you don't, then keep courage and hope and believe there will still be a way for us to reunite.

Best of luck!

With many kind regards and kisses, ·

Your faithful Ella.

P.S. I sent a birthday card to Lydi. Don't say anything about it.

1.8.49
Ottawa

My dear, dear Hans!

Your and my parents' birthday gifts arrived on Friday. My joy was overwhelming! And how beautiful they are! I await your next letter impatiently.

Greetings and kisses,

Ella.

5.8.49
Espelkamp
(received 12.8)

My dear Ella!

First of all, I apologize for my last two letters, which were very short. We waited and waited the last few weeks. Hope was dwindling, then, finally, there was clarity. The IRO distanced themselves from us and so everything fell apart for the time being. Mr. Klassen, on August 3rd, flew to America to clarify the matter. We will have to wait for the outcome. You also know how long this sort of thing takes from your own experience. So I considered moving from Gronau to Espelkamp. Here there is a group of Mennonites, Americans, Germans, and Dutch people, along with the 4 of us. It was organized by the MCC. Here in Espelkamp, a forest of 3 square kilometres and a former German Mennonite camp, a city for 10,000 inhabitants (refugees) is to be built.[92] *The Mennonites work here as volunteers. I came here because I wanted to see it, had heard a lot about it. Everything is still in its early stages. It is very beautiful here, like a health resort. All around is the forest, wonderful air. The food is American, a little unusual for us, but very good. For the time being, I'm happy to be out of the stable in Gronau.*

When the news came from the IRO, the mood was very sad. I was not at the meeting myself because I was on duty again, but everyone was so disappointed, including Siegfried Janzen. Some also howled in the Schützenhof. This time, it didn't affect me as much as it did when you went away and the decision came from London. Back then, I also had to fight the tears in my eyes that afternoon, though my colleague noticed it. This time, I hadn't expected too much. Now I did not know whether I should try to go back to Backnang immediately— maybe I could still get the job back. But it would not be nice if, after a while, some other possibility arose, and I had to leave the job again. I want to finally have a place of my own and know that I am at home and that I can stay there, with you. Because how can I start a family without a home? And because of our separation, it is even more difficult. If they don't get through to Canada, your parents want to try the United States, but, for now, there is nothing to be done. We have to wait and see what comes out of it. Hopefully they don't have to stay there for the winter, because it is very bad for one's health there, espe-cially for the children—the dust, that many people, crammed together, in such a small space. Backnang was like heaven in comparison. The Backnangers are afraid that many of us will want to go back, and that they will then have difficulties with the local authorities who do not want us to stay there. I want to try to learn more English. Maybe it is easier to learn here because I can speak English with the volunteers from America. Our warehouse consists only of a few wooden barracks, like at Maubacher Höhe. The MCC is housed in a barrack.

I often feel abandoned. I miss you, very much, as a comrade and person and friend. Sometimes, I also think of my little sister, who is now almost grown, 17 years old. Where is she! Sometimes I feel homesick for my parents. Yes, I

92   Peachey, Paul and Kurt Klaassen, *Espelkamp (Nordrhein-Westfalen, Germany)*, Global Anabaptist Mennonite Encyclopedia Online, last modified on August 23, 2013, at 14:00, https://gameo.org/index.php?title=Espelkamp_(Nordrhein-Westfalen,_Germany)&oldid=91723.

was a bad son and did not know how to treat my dear parents, but how does that help me now? If this is to be a punishment from God, I deserve it and have to bear it. Because there are some things in my life that shouldn't have been. I wish I could I be like these boys again and go back on the last 10 years of my life. But I cannot go back in time. What do you think? Should I go back to Backnang and try to start my own business? Mennonites are said to live here in Espelkamp. I want to take a closer look and inquire. For the time being, you cannot earn much here. If you got material to build here, I think you could build a house. Workers would be the MCC group. For the time being, the old stone barracks are being removed, I don't like them. But more about that later. If only could I hug you soon, forever, and not let go. This wait is an eternity for me!

A thousand kisses,

Your lonely Hans.

13.8.49
Ottawa

My dear, dear Hans!

Your first letter from Espelkamp reached me yesterday, and I thank you very much. Unfortunately, I haven't heard from my parents this week. They are likely too disappointed with the emigration. Sometimes, I think you have to come to grips with the idea of separation because, like C.F. Klassen said, this saga is difficult and now is the darkest time. But we, Hans, don't want to give up hope, we trust God's guidance and each other, do we not? If my parents want to go to America, we may not reunite. But what do we humans know? Sometimes, I think I'm not a good daughter, either, because I went off to Canada and left my parents alone. Isn't there a possibility for Volksdeutsche? I quietly hope that the Lord will answer our prayers and this time it will work. It should.

I often think of your parents and sister, wherever they may be. They are certainly also concerned about you, if they are alive. I understand you so well in this—now, much better than before. But we are separated! You know, if we do get together, which I still hope for, in spite of myself, being, for the first time, alone, in a foreign country, without parents, alongside strangers, is useful for building inner strength. I will be a good comrade for you. You have a hard time behind you. But I think we will get along well and, together, we will survive the struggle of life.

With an overflowing heart,

Your Ella.

19.8.49

My dear Ella!

The past week has been very long for me, a week without mail from you! Every day, when I got home from work, I always checked, and my face grew longer every day. Your mom sent me your dear letter from August 1 only this week, because she has had much to do with the children. Your father is in the hospital—he had an operation on the tonsils. Your parents are very nice people. I like them, and they like me, as do your siblings—especially Hardi. They were very nice to me and we got on very well. Your father also told me to emigrate alone if it comes to it. I also take it for granted that they will emigrate without me if need be, because they are your family and you are over there. Canada, as you can see, is not exactly enthusiastic about the Mennonites, but workers are needed. We don't know if all of this was the last word. But it seems to me that the outcome was not very favourable—otherwise, Mr. Klassen would not be back from the States so quickly. Otherwise, he would have already announced something in Gronau. Yes, Ella, we want to continue to hope and trust. Because in the future, a lot will depend on this, too—our reunion, if we want it. If your parents don't get through, you might think about coming back. I don't know whether you would just for me. I'm afraid to ask this question, because I don't know what your decision would be. It is too early to decide but maybe, one day, the decision will have to be made. Dear Ella, maybe it shouldn't come to that, but tell me, what can we humans, who are so weak, do about it? Our destinies are guided by God. We know nothing. I am grateful that I met you, but I understand what is bothering you, maybe more today than ever before. And I am deeply in your debt. But tell me, dearest - if you or I would have sailed in September, we would not have gotten engaged, because we were not yet sure about it. I am grateful for the beautiful days of Christmas in Thomashof, even if they were just moments, because they showed us we understand each other. Yes, today, I, and maybe you, know we shouldn't have parted, though it may also have been God's way. Today, I am ready to say that a girl will never mean more to me than my Ella. There is no danger I will become unfaithful to you. I have asked myself and came to this conclusion. And if it should be that we don't come together again, I will not come close to any other girl.

I am glad that you also think of my relatives. I think my mother would also be very good to you, and you would understand each other very well. I would have been very proud to introduce you to her. You are very similar to her in character, because you think more about others than yourself. My mother had to go through a lot during the difficult time in Russia and yet, she was always brave. If she lives today, she surely worries a lot. Maybe my parents reunited, if they got through the bad years. Sometimes, I think of my little sister, who is now 17 years old. I couldn't even pray for my family when the Russians came, because then, I didn't believe in God. If this is also a punishment for that, I will bear it. Well, I first want to hear what news Klassen brings, then we'll see. Just keep your head up, and don't lose your courage. The sun will shine for us, too. And, if you think about it, some are much worse off. I just think of my loved ones in Siberia. The prospects are not so bright in Germany, though, either. But our situation will become clearer with time!

A thousand hugs and kisses,

Your Hans.

P.S. I let my beard grow. What do you think? Should I shave it off again, or should I send you a picture of it? Included is one from Gronau.

20.8.49
Ottawa

My dear Hans, my "grandpa"!

It is 1/2 before 10 in the evening and I have just finished my work. It is already quite dark outside, and there are stars in the sky and silence all around, so I would like to chat with my Hans. I think, with horror, on how long we have been apart, and the future feels blacker than ever. But, right now, I have the feeling that everything will be fine. That we will definitely get together. Why shouldn't we reunite? You will say, you can keep hope: you are in Canada, now, while I sit in the camp, with uncertainty, little hope, and no money. Is that so? Though we were actually together for a very short time, our thoughts and feelings are so closely connected. I got to know you better, dearest, through our letters, and I love you more and more the longer we are apart. I would not have thought that my love for you would get stronger with us being apart for so long.

For me, the separation and isolation (if I am to be honest) are big troubles. But it is good to get away from home first, gain some experience, and then think about the next serious step. You already had some time on your own. Could you have crafted a life together with the young Ella from Backnang? Or do you doubt yourself with today's Ella? Honestly, Hans, haven't you changed a bit also in the meantime? Believe in us, our wish and dream will be fulfilled!

You ask, "What will you do if your parents come over and I don't, or vice versa?!" I got a letter from mom, in which she asked what they should do if it doesn't work out for them to go to Canada or the US—whether they should go to Uruguay or whether I'd want to come back. For the time being, I do not have to make a decision, because our cause is not entirely hopeless. In the meantime, I'm going to finish my contract and try to settle into life here, while you try to find something there. Don't forget, Hans, the thought of Canada, otherwise I'll forget you! Everything mutual! When I received your letter about the rejection from London, I had a difficult, lonely day. My lonely Hans, how I would like to drive away your loneliness and see you laugh again. But it's not up to me, my best comrade!

Looking forward to your next letter, and to hear what you have done and what your plans are. I am glad that you have good food to eat. Enjoy it, and get your strength back!

Warmly, with kisses,

Your bride-to-be.

27.8.49
Espelkamp

My dear little one, my dear Ella!

Today, I want to pick up my pen again, to chat a little with you. I don't have a nice little letter from you in front of me, but it's my fault—last time, I made you wait. My dear girl, you are not angry with me because of my questions that I asked you in my last letter, are you? There are so many problems that have arisen. I always want everything to be open between us, as it was from the beginning. Your next letter, which may already be on its way, will give me an answer to a number of things.

I'm still here in Espelkamp, but I'm already thinking about where to go next. Today, I wrote to ask my boss in Backnang whether they would be willing to take me back. How things stand with the emigration is not yet clear, but I hardly believe that something will come this year. I would like to make some money again, if it's going to take months. I am considering your help. Maybe you can sponsor me when your year is over, if you still believe in me. You can decide this now. It may be a lot of trouble, but I think it is pretty much the only way. In terms of money, I think it could work if we get help from my aunt. I would then try as a Volksdeutsche. The other problem would be housing and work, I think it would be better if we went to Winnipeg or wherever there are more Mennonites. All of this is not easy and may be too much for you. Please write me what you think about it. If I can't go to Backnang, which I would like, because of the work and the company (maybe you can come to me, too), I will have to look for something in Gronau. If I travelled to the Volksdeutsche Lager, which is now in Bremen, it will not take too long until it is decided—about 2 weeks—but the costs are borne by the emigrants, or by relatives overseas. Now I have to wait and see what you write to me.

Would you be happy, dear Ella, if I came over now to join our paths together, or would it be too fast for you? In this one year, you have had time to get to know life a little. You are not sorry that you met me, are you? I am grateful that our paths crossed, and we fell in love. For me, it is more than what I have lost. Now, I ask you to forgive me if I have written you something you don't like, or if I have hurt you. We bear each other's burdens. I wish I could relieve you of the concerns about your loved ones. But dearest Ella, don't lose heart. One day, the sun will shine for us.

With many, many kisses,

Your faraway Hans.

2.9.49
Ottawa

My dear Hans!

Above all, please excuse me that I am only replying now to the letters of August 19th and 27th. I'm sure you've been waiting for an answer. This evening, I finished work quite late, as we had a cocktail party; there were 10 people, including the commanding general for Europe in World War II.[93] My people are very nice to me. I'm so glad I'm here in Ottawa. So the important thing first: I am happy to sponsor you. I had written so to you before, and have not changed my mind. I want to do my best to bring you over. The prospects in Germany are not good, and it would be better if you came here. Do you think I should work to the end of my contract first, though? That would be 5 months! During this time, I would be able to save the travel money, if I didn't spend anything. But if I could sponsor you sooner, I would still be ready to complete my contract if necessary, don't you think? Would you have something against that? The main thing is for you to be here. But I can also pay $12 a month and be free from my contract. But there is still time to decide. And what do you mean by locating in Winnipeg or where other

---

93   It is unclear if Ella may be referring to the Supreme Allied Commander General of the Army Dwight D. Eisenhower or General Harry Crerar, First Canadian Army.

Mennonites are? Say dearest, don't you want to be where I am? I am hoping we can still switch. And when I completed my year, I'm free. I don't know how it is with you. I preferred Ottawa at the beginning, because I am well-known here and believe it would be easier for me to find work and accommodations here. I assume that the Martin family and, through them, the people in the church, would help me. Don't you think that would be best? Finding a place to live and work in strange places through strangers is difficult. I think it would be better to try here. The main thing is that you get here. Then, we can choose where we intend to establish ourselves. I would also like to be near Mennonites, in Winnipeg or Kitchener. I think we'd come to an agreement. What do you think? Today, I cannot say how I would choose. I have to think about it and inquire. Poor boy, you have to wait so long! Yes, I still think we'll reunite. I still have the possibility to return to you if you still love me. But, you know, maybe I won't get a visa?! Oh, yes, with all the bitter seriousness, something must be fun, right? But if it should take longer, it would be better if you would earn some money.

Kisses, from one country to another,

Your Ella.

3.9.49
Espelkamp
(received 9.9)

My dear Ella, my dear bride-to-be!

Another week has passed. First of all, thank you very much for your letter from August 20ᵗʰ, which gave me great pleasure. I can see that I mean as much to you as I did before—maybe even more. And, when I hope to read our letters together later, we will surely see we wrote on the same day and had the same thoughts. Isn't it nice that we feel the same, even if we are thousands of kilometres apart?! Only in one thing do I not agree with you. I am not without hope. Uncertainty and worries, a little bit, yes, but I hold firm. Trust that everything will be fine with the two of us. And, as far as money is concerned: it is a minor matter. I still have 100 marks set aside in reserve. Today, I got a 10-mark pension payment and earned 9 marks with photos. In addition, I worked one and a half hours on a building every evening this week and that earned me a few marks, too. Well, I haven't given up on Canada completely, since you are there, let's give it a try. It also depends on what your parents want to do. If they want to stay here, you will have to decide.

Your letters are very precious to me, and I am happy every time a new one comes. I wish I had one every day. But, of course, you can't, because you have too much work and too little free time. I am more than happy when something comes from you. Once we are together and if we do not get along sometimes, which I hope won't happen, we should take our letters and look at what we wrote to each other, and we will surely work it out. What do you think, my love, my Ella?

During the war, I had a comrade, Franz Bayerl, from Vienna who kept his wife's letters in a folder. And when he had the time, he took them out and "read the Bible," as he called it. When the Russians set fire to his car, his book was burned, and he was inconsolable. Another of my comrades was loyal to his wife throughout the years, in Poland, France, and Russia. When the war was over, he couldn't stand it any longer, and escaped from captivity. He was caught and sent to France, where he had to stay for a few more years. I always wished I would have a woman that I could love so much.

Incidentally, my nickname is now Hans Bart[94], for distinguishing between us here, as we have 4 Hanses. Goodbye, until next time. In the meantime, I have become really active. I just helped wash dishes, which I learned here. Pretty good, don't you think?! Sending a kiss to my little bride-to-be.

Auf Wiedersehn!

Your Hans.

Johann "Hans Bart" in Espelkamp 1949.

....

94   Bart is the German word for beard. Johann grew a beard in Espelkamp.

6.9.49
Ottawa

My dear fiancé, my dear Hans!

Since I made you wait so long the last time, I want to start writing today. Soon, you will have my letter in your hands, while I, this time, will probably have to wait a little longer for mail. But don't make me wait too long! I don't have too much time to write, but always am reading and thinking. I will try everything to get you over here but, if it doesn't work, I'm more for southern Germany. I'm curious what AEG will tell you. Mom wrote me that they want to try going to the US. I hope we can be together, because they will have particular difficulties with the language. But in the long run, that would be better than living in a camp. How I wish you dear ones, you and my relatives, were here. But be patient, this day is coming!

Good night, my dear! Sleep well.

9.9.49
Ottawa

My dear Hans (Bart)!

Today, your dear letter from September 3 came, and I received it with great joy and gratitude. Mr. Martin already says he can find farm work for my parents and you near Kitchener-Waterloo. But for you, I'd prefer a factory. He said that there are 4 factories in Elmira—for furniture and other things. His son is in Kitchener and could help us, too. It is fine that you want to send me a picture with your beard, you Hans-Bart. Would I like it? I somewhat doubt it. First, I want to see your picture, then I'll judge. What have you and my parents decided?

Your Ella.

13.9.49
Espelkamp
(received 19.9)

My dear Ella!

This time, it took me a little longer to reply. Please excuse me. I wanted to write you more about my plans. So, it didn't work out with Backnang—the business is not going very well there. Now, it's time to look around. Today, we went to a job centre in Lütbeche. It is very unfavourable, with little industry— all agriculture. There, we were told there was no work.

Now, about emigration. Please inquire at the immigration office as to how you can sponsor me and explain how things are with me. I think we can tell them everything truthfully, because the difficulties no longer exist as they did before. I think it is better that you complete your contract, because it will still take several months. A week ago, I was in Gronau, talking to your parents. They want to keep going, but your father finds it difficult to sit there without work. I felt like I was going home to Gronau, because I know your parents like me. But I don't want to go back there myself. It's still the same as before; nothing has changed in the time I was gone. Hardi is still as wild as ever. He had fallen out of a car again and hit his head, but looks good otherwise. He had a lot of fun with my beard, and asked me if everyone grew a beard where I was. Of course, I told him that if he came there, he would grow one, too, but he didn't really believe me. Some didn't recognize me in the camp. I shaved it off today. Still, it's good to have some fun during this serious time. Now, I look younger again. Beyond this, I'm fine. I think I've gotten pretty strong. Hopefully, I will get a job soon, so that I can earn something again. What should I buy first? Maybe a black suit? What do you think? Don't forget your Hans completely!

With a lot of kisses that I save for seeing you again,

Your Hans.

22.9.49
Gronau
(received 1.10)

My dear Ella!

Yesterday, I was interviewed by the work commission. Your relatives did the same today, but, of course, the big end is yet to come. It will be decided in a few weeks. Until then, patience, dear child! As you can see, I landed in Gronau again. It came as a surprise. On Saturday, the telegram came to Espelkamp. On Monday, we left. It was very difficult for us to say goodbye to the MCC volunteers. They had liked us, and we them. There was lots of good camaraderie. Now, we have landed in our stable again. The first thing we received here was air too thick to cut (I enclose a picture of it, though the dust and stench and noise cannot, of course, be seen). But maybe we will get through it in 2-3 weeks. New people come every day. It is fuller than before. If I can't get through now, let's try again via Bremen by you sponsoring me—then, we'll see. I hope, at least, that your parents will get through this time—then, you won't be alone anymore. Oh, to finally have a homeland and a home! Maybe we have to go through all of this to appreciate what we have at home. I believe that home will always be my favourite place. Just don't worry little Ella, the possibility that I will become a General no longer exists and so I would not drag you from one reception to another! I thought a lot about you in the evening. Hope to write you more next week. Stay healthy.

With a lot of kisses, I remain yours,

Hans.

26.9.49
Gronau
(received 1.10)

My dear Ella!

Again, I have to apologize for the short letter, but I think you'll forgive me. I hope it will still make you happy—perhaps more than all the other letters together. I was before the Commission today and flew through—it was over in 20 minutes.

But not as usual. It all happened so quickly that I only came to my senses when I was outside. So, my dear Ellalein, I'm coming! I will tell you everything else when we can look each other in the eyes again. I just want to tell you that it was the same consul who gave me his word in Ludwigsburg. So I was lucky, if only a year later. He recognized me immediately. As per usual, one is lucky and the other is not. I hope and pray that your parents can get through, too. I have God to thank. I wasn't as scared, this time, as back then, in Ludwigsburg. I no longer had such a great desire to emigrate. If you weren't there, I wouldn't at all, but everything will come as it should. Now, I want to put my things in order here. I am very, very glad that I will see you soon. Write to me as soon as you receive this letter. Maybe I'll get an answer in time. All the best until we see each other again. The last interview is behind me!

'Til we see each other soon, my lovely, little, dark-haired Ella!

Your Hans.

P.S. The ship is expected to leave on Oct. 13.

27.9.49
Ottawa

My dear Hans!

I was grateful to receive your dear letter from September 13. As you said, there is nothing in Backnang. Yes, I can imagine that the news of your beard ran like wildfire through the camp. There, at least, they had a little change from the ordinary. Please don't grow a full beard. You think you don't need to shave, then? Yes, tell me, do you still want to come to Canada, when the Canadian dollar has fallen so much? Living is actually expensive here—1 spool of thread costs 15 cents. A small, furnished room rents for $25. I can't tell you anything about the emigration yet, as I want to go to the office on Friday. Nice that you feel at home with my parents, and about dear little Hardi's interest in your beard! Must have been funny!

Sending you warm regards from over the sea,

Your Ella.

1.10.49
Ottawa

My dear Hans!

Just received your two dear letters, from September 22 and 26, with the happy news that you got through! I cannot tell you how happy I am. Sorry about the writing. I'm in a great hurry and excitement. My employers will soon be here, at noon, but I want so much, dearest, to have these lines still reach you—hopefully, in good health. Also hope that it works with my parents. Glory to the Lord God and thank Him for getting you through! He answered our prayers. I'm really looking forward to seeing you again and hope that you will come through Ottawa. Where are you going, British Columbia? I want my parents to come through Ottawa, if they get through.

I would like to express a wish. I would like you to buy me a black handbag before you come, because here it is $40. Buy yourself a suit! But that's all a minor matter. The main thing is that you come! If you have enough money, an expensive camera would also be great, which you could now get! Now, I wish you a good crossing! Write me from the ship, too!

See you soon!

Love to my parents and siblings!

Your Ella.

1.10.49
Ottawa

Though I hurriedly wrote a few lines to you today, I will write you some more, because this is probably the last letter that will still reach you in Germany. You know, dearest, it didn't seem possible to me that you would get through, because I had very little hope. I very much hope that my parents are lucky, too. Thank you for the picture of the camp warehouse. You will soon have this abnormal life behind you and will be on to a foreign land. Do you know where you will be settled? Since I hope you will make a stop in Ottawa, I would like to give you a phone number where you can reach me. And if my parents can't get through, please ask just for a few dollars on my behalf, so you can write to me from the ship and then when you arrive in Canada. I can pick you up at the train station. This will be a reunion, after almost 10 months of separation! I'm really looking forward to it. But my employers will be alarmed that I plan to leave. It won't harm anything—perhaps they'll may pay more. If you get to meet the Martin family, don't be surprised: they are not European. I was very disappointed yesterday to hear that these types of Mennonites don't have much of a Christmas tree, that would be 'worldly.' Your mood on the ship, Samaria, will probably be different than mine at that time. Just don't get seasick! Will you have something to say to me when you see me? Because I have a lot stored up!!!

Many warm regards and kisses, for the last time, across the sea!

Looking forward to seeing you,

Your Ella

International Refugee Organization (IRO) Certificate, Amalie Rupp, Lydia, Bernhard.

International Refugee Organization (IRO) Certificate. Johann Rupp.

Johann Franz's crate, briefcase, and camera equipment.

Johann Franz (L) and Arthur Kroeger (R) on "S.S. Samaria" October 1949.

Undated
(received 7.10.49)

My dear Ella!

The letter in which I informed you that I have the visa is already in your hands. Today, I can also give you the happy news that your parents passed the commission, too. Now we are very excited for our next move. Though I wrote the ship would depart on October 13th, we will probably leave next Thursday or Friday. When you have waited as long as we have, things end up going too fast, and you have to hurry to get everything done. My guarantor is in Headingley, Manitoba, said to be 40 miles from Winnipeg. Your parents do not yet know where they are going, but have been promised they will be near Winnipeg, too. When you complete your year there, I hope you will also come to Winnipeg. Then, we will not be as far apart as we are now and can see each other. Maybe my farmer will release me sooner. Mr. R. Rupp is already in Winnipeg, and likes it there very much. All our acquaintances are coming together there. Hope you will be fine with it, too. I received your letter from September 27 on September 30. I thought maybe something had happened. I hope to see you soon, darling, in Canada!

Hans.

12.10.49
Bremen
(received 20.10)

My dear Ella!

Now I want to write you the last letter from Europe. The emigration will take us to Cuxhaven tomorrow at 8 a.m. From there it goes to Quebec. I don't know when we will land there—you may know it earlier. Had to go through the consul and doctor today and yesterday. We left the baggage this morning— just have to pack a suitcase for tomorrow, then I'm done. I've already written the last letters. Only one more night, then the big journey begins.

Tomorrow, it will be exactly two years since I came to Germany. Now I'm leaving, probably with feelings significantly different than the ones you had when you left. For you went abroad to a foreign land, while I am going to my new homeland, because my dear, little, dark Ella is waiting for me there. I received your most recent letter at the very last moment, before leaving. When I ask Hardi, where are you going? He says, To my Ella! I ask, And where is she? He says, In America! To my Ella! Now, we have the last few hours in Germany. Everything I do, I think, for the last time in Germany. Now, I want to end my letter, the last one in Germany. Looking forward to seeing my Ella again! Many, many kisses hurry toward you across the sea!

Your Hans.

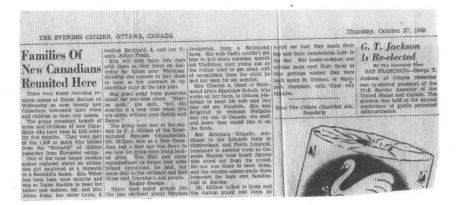

Families of New Canadians Reunited Here

Thursday, October 27, 1949 THE EVENING CITIZEN, OTTAWA, CANADA:
"Families of New Canadians Reunited Here"

There were many touching reunion scenes at Union Station on Wednesday as over twenty new Canadians welcomed their wives and children to their new homes.

The group consisted largely of wives and children of new Canadians who have been in this country five months. They were part of the 1,200 or more who landed from the "Samaria" at Quebec yesterday from European camps.

One of the most happy reunion scenes centred about an attractive girl employed as a domestic in a Rockcliffe home. Ella Weber has been here nine months and was at Union Station to meet her father and mother, Mr. and Mrs. Johan Rupp, her sister Lydia, 9, brother Bernhard, 4, and her fiancé, Johan Franz.

Ella will only have two days with them as they leave on Saturday for farms near Winnipeg. However she expects to join them as soon as her contract is up, sometime early in the new year.

She shied away from questions about her marriage plans. "Maybe soon", she said, "but ten months is a long time when you are alone, without your family and fiancé."

The group was met at the station by C.J. Millner of the International Refugee Organization. Mr. Millner, who as a New Canadian just a year ago was down to see how the group was being looked after. The IRO and other organizations no longer look after inland operations, he said, but leave that to the railways and Red Cross and Traveller's Aid people.

... There were two lonely figures who stood out from the crowd. No one was there to meet them, and the reunion scenes made them homesick for their own families, still in Europe.

Mr. Millner talked to them and the station guard told them he would see that they made their bus and train connections later in the day. But home-sickness was written large over their faces as they perhaps wished they were back again in Gronau, or Stuttgart, Germany, with their own families.[95]

29.10.49
Ottawa

My dear Hans!

I do not know whether I will send this letter, since it may not be very encouraging. And yet, I still want to put my thoughts of today on paper. The reunion is over. It was actually just a moment, like a dream, over so quickly. I saw you the last time just 2 days ago and yet an eternity! I'm already counting the days until I see you again, but I would love to come to you today! Are you feeling the same as me? This time, I'm the one who stayed behind, like you did in Backnang. This afternoon, I had the blues. But it cannot be changed. I have to hope for the next reunion. If you had a job for me, I could come to you soon. If not, I want to use the 3 months to put things in order. Do you know what's

....

95   "Families of New Canadians Reunited Here", *The Evening Citizen*, Ottawa, Canada, Thursday, October 27, 1949, accessed on microfim (inter-library loan) at the Red Deer Public Library.

on my cupboard? The Bearded Hans and the "Samaria" that brought you to Canada.

All my thoughts and wishes still belong to you,

Your Ella.

30.10.49
Headingley

My dear, dear Ella!

Although I'm not quite there yet, I want to start a letter to you because I have time and want to take advantage of it. We arrived safely here today. The farmer sponsoring your parents was a little late. We looked around the station and I spoke to a gentleman in English, who then phoned Mr. Borne. Had a little chat and then a young man suddenly came and asked for the name of your father. It was Borne's son. He took us to a certain Mr. Esau, from whom he borrowed the car. The last part of the way, about 3 1/2 miles long, your parents had to go by horse carriage, because the way was too dirty for the car. Mr. Esau went to Winnipeg. When he comes back, he will bring me to my farmer, who lives about 10 miles further west. The trip on the train went very well. We didn't see much, only forest and rocks. For Hardi, it was taking too long; in the last hour before we reached Winnipeg, he was always asking how much further it was.

You know, dearest Ella, I like you even better now than in Backnang, although I liked you there, too. If you were a man, I would say that you have become more masculine during this time, but I have to express myself otherwise and say you have become womanlier. When I was over there, I often thought about what my Ella would look like when I could hug her. You have more poise, now, and I think you have also become a little more serious during this time. I sat on the train and dreamed of my Ella, my little bride-to-be. I am glad that I could see you and that the wait for a reunion did not take years. And I'm longing for the moment we'll always be together. I don't deserve this happiness, but I believe that if He has brought us to a country where we are no longer separated by water, it will be His will that we come together. I said to Mr.

Martin when I saw the sun go down behind the St. *Lawrence River* on Sunday evening that the whole country in the west was lit up, that *Canada* lay ahead of us. This morning the train rocked again, as if we should be reminded of the troubled times and years behind us.

31.10.49

Today I have now arrived at *Mr. Siemens's*. Imagine—to my surprise, he is Harry Giesbrecht's uncle. *Victor G.* was just here. The people are very nice and my first impression was good. I don't see any work here for me, but I'll get work, in town. *Mr. Siemens* advises me very much to work off my contract. For the time being he wants to keep me with him until I find a job. I believe that it will be the most sensible thing to hold out through this year. Even if I earn less, it is better for the future. *We* want to stay in *Canada* and have to think ahead.

I don't know how your parents have made out yet. It was very dirty here yesterday but has frozen since. You have to adjust at first, but it will be fine. *As* for our future, I believe that as soon as you have your year completed, you should come here, and we will get married as soon as possible. *Will* you, dearest *Ella*? Once my time is completed, we could look for where we will settle. Harry already has his own car. There are a lot of acquaintances in *Winnipeg*. Goodnight, my dear little bride-to-be, dream of me, which I will of you. I'm sending you kisses, and thinking of my most glorious girl who exists on earth. *We'll* be together soon.

Your Hans.

2.11.49
Ottawa

My dear Hans! Thank you very much for your first letter in *Canada*. *Already* you have met acquaintances. *As* you write, your farmer has no work for you. Hopefully you will find an acceptable position. *Do* you have to work out your contract in the countryside? *Maybe* you could work in the hospital in *Winnipeg*? Or would you not want to? I don't know if it's possible

136

anyway. All of this is beside the point; the main thing is that you are in Canada, that a year will go by. You know, I didn't know that men, even if they get married, have to complete their year of immigration service. So only women have the right to stop.

After you left Ottawa, it was a bit sad for me to stay behind. I was a little tired on Friday, but I went to school. Saturday was a difficult day for me. I worked mechanically; my thoughts were with you. So many questions came up. I don't have any news from my parents yet, but I hope they haven't found it too bad. And now you're not even together. I hope my parents get over the difficult start well. Don't take it too hard yourself; this time will also pass. And always keep your head up.

I was happy to read your lines and that you still like me. I would very much like to respond to your suggestion and come to you after my contract. I'm looking forward to seeing you again, for a longer time. It was too short, wasn't it? But after thinking about it, I decided the best thing would be to stay here until then. I am doing very well. And when I think of you, on the other hand, I know it is not so easy on a farm. I'd like to help the Martin family in the shop until Christmas. But more than that which keeps me here, my groom is drawing me away. I will probably come to Manitoba in mid-February. Until then, I still have a lot to do. To answer your question, it's a "YES!" Now, we will want to be very thrifty.

I pray for your loved ones, too. Maybe, God willing, you will get a message. I dreamed of your Mom last night. Where it was, I don't know; maybe Canada, because she was a domestic servant. And there was a little girl like your sister. I went to visit and you introduced me to her for the first time and were immediately sympathetic toward one another. If only it hadn't been a dream. Do you know which pictures are now on my desk? The ship that brought my Hans over the ocean and Hans Bart! I like this picture very much. In your eyes, there is such confidence and trust in God. You know that I can say of you that you have become more masculine, even though you were already, in Backnang. But in our hearts we want to be like children, don't we?

Your Ella.

9.11.49
Headingley

My dearest girl!

Unfortunately, I am only able to answer the precious letter of yours I received on Monday today. On Monday, I was very tired and I wanted to go to bed earlier, because on Tuesday, Mr. Siemens went to deliver cattle to the slaughterhouse and we had to get up earlier than usual. I wanted to write Tuesday evening, then, but Mr. Esau came to get me. We had agreed that he wouldn't come get me until Saturday, but he came earlier. I will probably stay here for 3-4 weeks. We will harvest beets if it does not start to rain. Beyond this, there is nothing to do because of the mud. I drove the beets out of the field with horses today—a little unusual, but it works. I've gotten used to work at Mr. Siemens's a little, and it is not too difficult for me anymore. My first job was a huge pile of wood that I chopped into small pieces, and I also helped in the barn: feeding cattle, mucking out manure, and milking. I was assigned to drive the milk machine back and forth and wash it out. I have already learned something. Today, I tried to milk by hand, but that still needs to be learned. Esau's 11-year-old son watched me, and said I milked like a hen, but no master has yet fallen from heaven. Will hold out as long as possible. Don't worry, I'm not going to give up. The main thing is to stay healthy, and then, everything will be fine.

The food is very good, here, and you eat your fill. Don't know if you would care for me right now, if you saw me. Sometimes I stink of crap. I don't mind myself, I am a farm worker. And the main thing is that I earn some money, because I don't want to sit around. Time flies very quickly; today, I looked through the calendar and saw I've been in Canada 15 days already. Half an hour ago, I spoke to your parents. They asked me if I had already become a "mister".[96] Yes! They want to move to Winnipeg, now; hopefully your Papa will find a job. In autumn, it can be hard, because a lot of people go to the city from the countryside. It would be easier in spring. As for me, I want to work off my contract as much as possible. It is better for the future. I have to keep thinking ahead.

....

96   Mist is the German word for manure.

I'm really excited that you want to come to Manitoba in mid-February. If you get here in time for my birthday, I think it will prove the most beautiful, since I will turn a quarter of a century. Time flies. Next year, my dear, little, sweet Ella will be of full age, and thus grown. But, you know, darling, you are still very smart for your age, and I am very proud of my Ella. These few months are not an eternity. Hopefully you will not forget me during this time. We will spend this Christmas and New Year's alone, but the next ones together, and every other one, too! At New Year's we will have been engaged one year! And I only saw you once during this time. But how beautiful were the hours that I could spend with you—they passed like in a dream. Isn't it nice that we still understand each other exactly as before, maybe even better?

You know, darling, I've organized all your letters by date, and when I long for you, I read them, and you speak to me. How far away are those long lines when you had left Europe and I got the rejection? All of this speaks from your letters: memories, love, hope, doubt and faith. There are already 38 letters. Unfortunately, the mail is too slow here, too. Is there no airmail between Winnipeg and Ottawa? Write to me diligently. I am still waiting for the mail, just as before. But come in February, too! If your parents are in Winnipeg, you can stay with them for the first while. We will find work. We will make it together.

Now I want to close for today. Tomorrow, it's back in the beets! I have two beautiful horses that pull well. I would like to see Hardi. Your Mom told me on the phone that he is no longer leaving the stable. I would like to see him again on the farm. It's really a shame they are going to the city. It would be better for the children if they stayed in the country.

Kisses,

Your impatient Hans.

My dear Hans!

Today, I received your dear letter from November 9th with great joy. Yesterday was "Remembrance Day" and there was, unfortunately, no mail from you, dearest, nor my parents nor the dear Rundschau. If you want the mail to go quickly, it costs 7 cents for airmail stamps. So I always want to do it that way. Do it that way, too, then I'll get mail from you faster, and you will, from me, too. The mail is also too slow for me!

I can see from your letter that you are very tired and have it really hard. Much harder than me. I'm very proud of you! My Hans has a strong will and will successfully pass through this difficult transition period. So, you are already learning to milk! Well, by the time I get there you will be a real farmer, huh? You know, in my opinion, you shouldn't be so committed to the year. You could also look for work in Winnipeg. If Mr. Esau only needs you for 3-4 weeks, it might be worth it. You could ask Mr. Siemens to let you go freely and, after 1 year, issue a certificate to say you worked there, because, in the spring, it will be difficult to stop work in the country. It's said that changing positions is not a good thing, but it's not noted on the certificate at the end of the contract. I don't want to change your mind, though; maybe it's better to endure. I just want you to have it easier.

This Christmas will be my first without my parents. How long have you been alone? Yes, dearest, I'm also looking forward to being with you, because we have really had very little time together. It is very convenient that my parents are now in Winnipeg and maybe I'll take a job sewing. I'm not worried; women can find work more easily. I have determined I will be there for your birthday. This is an important birthday! 25 years! And mine, too, of legal age! The past 3-4 years have passed very quickly. And the long months apart have been crossed out on the calendar, because now you are here.

Last Sunday, at the Martin family's, we debated, the two of us. Jake said we should wait a few more years to get married, until we have had a chance of establishing ourselves. He's not entirely wrong, but . . . . I totally agree with you. If we see each other again after a few months, we can see clearly and talk about it then. I'll be there in February, for sure! I'm really, really looking forward to it.

For today, warm regards and kisses,

Your Ella.

P.S. You certainly changed quickly to "John Franz"!

16.11.49
Headingley

My dearest Ella, my dear bride-to-be!

Today, I received your precious letter from November 12, with great pleasure, at the same time as the book. I want to answer today, so that you get the letter soon. I would like to speak to you every evening but, unfortunately, it is not possible. But I am looking forward to the time when it will be. Basically, I am lonely here; I spend the evenings by myself. The people are not very talkative, but I don't mind. I have never imposed myself on anyone. What I like here is that we sit down for dinner at 6 p.m., and then I have the evening for myself. Now I have gotten used to the work. I did sweat a lot for the first few days but I just kept reminding myself that even the longest day comes to an end. It is not particularly good to work in the fields this time of year. Last night, it snowed, then melted today—a lot of mud—the machines got stuck, so we had to load by hand. Yesterday, we loaded 8 trucks by hand. Today, we used the loader. Then, with the chain, I drove out a load of wood for the beet workers (Poles) sleeping in so-called cabooses on the field. Then, I fed the cattle and started milking. Then the afternoon was done. The days are getting shorter now, and as soon as the snow sticks to the ground, the beets will be done. Don't be worried, for me, about the heavy work. Who knows what might happen?

I was back in Winnipeg last Sunday. It's a shame, your parents were here that evening. But I didn't get home until late, so I haven't seen them at all yet. I visited Mrs. Friesen, who was with my mother when they fled from Russia.

I also spoke to a Mrs. Isaak, who was with my mother in Hohensalza[97] just before the Russians came. When I am around people like this, I always have the feeling that I might find my loved ones. That's my biggest concern now. Sometimes, I am homesick, too. Last Monday it was particularly hard on my heart. If I didn't have you, it would be very difficult for me.

Don't worry about me, it's not so difficult that I'm too tired in the evening to pick up a book and learn something. But I have little dealings with English speakers. Besides me, there are 2 boys here. One understands Ukrainian and the other Plattdeutsch[98]. But the difficulty with the language will be overcome. Most have learned English immigrating here.

With my first pay cheque, I'll probably have to buy something warm to wear. I have a parka in mind (do you know what that is?) and a pair of rubber boots with fur on the inside. My coat is too light here. Mr. Siemens bought me a pair of felt boots with galoshes. I have already bought a pair of leather gloves to work with. I'm very happy because, otherwise, I would always have to dig through the dirt with my hands.

That's enough for now; I want to learn some more English tonight. The boss comes tomorrow morning. We will put up some hay. Goodnight, my dear Ella, I hope you will dream of me as I will of you!

Lots of kisses,

Your Hans.

P.S. Don't worry about the name John, my aunt has always written to me in Germany like this. That is my formal name. To you, I am the old Hans, as I am to my old friends.

....

97   Hohensalza is now known as Inowroclaw, Poland.

98   Plattdeutsch, also known as Plautdietsch, is the Mennonite Low German dialect.

19.11.49
Ottawa

My dear Hans!

Thank you for your lovely letter. As I can see from your lines, you are willing to stay to the end of your contract. It is probably better that way; 1 year is not an eternity. You may find it more difficult because of the wound, but I am sure you will make it if you stay healthy. It is colder where you are than it is here, and I can understand that it is not very pleasant to work outside in the field. You know, I participated in a beet harvest in the Russian zone. It was just a small field and was also done by hand. You will soon have to stop this work because of the cold. You, dear Hans, Mom wrote me that you were an administrator on an English farm and there would be a lot of cattle, is that right? Esau, isn't that a Mennonite name? You are writing about 3-4 weeks, but now do you think you can stay on?

I am sorry, dear Jonny, but I don't know what the word "parka" means. I have looked in my dictionary but don't find this word at all. I assume it's a warm jacket. Right? I received something for the cold yesterday from Mrs. Martin: warm overshoes, brown and hardly worn. I am very happy with them. Now I'm afraid that my coat will be too thin, but I won't be spending much of the winter in Manitoba. That you have little opportunity to speak English with others is very unfortunate, because you have a special talent with languages. Mrs. Martin praised your pronunciation highly. I am really proud of you.

I understand your homesickness for your loved ones very well. Now that we've been apart, I've learned to appreciate mine a lot more, and I'm so glad they are now in Canada. How nice it would be for you to know yours are safe. Soon, soon your Ella is coming to Winnipeg! Continue to write to me about your work, because I am interested in everything! And don't be unfaithful to me!

We now have a headache over my employers' daughter's dance. She'll be at a ball in Montreal next Friday and will even be introduced to the

Governor-General.[99] *My employers have just returned; the garage is below and I can hear them. I wish you continued good health. God bless and be with you!*

Your Ella.

22.11.49
Headingley

My dear Ella!

Today, I received your dear letter from November 19th with much joy and thanks. I transported straw around today. I had to wait a while on the way, because the road was not free, and I was able to finish reading your letter. You ask what we do. Now, at 10 to 6, it is up early in the morning, first feeding the cattle and harnessing horses in the barn. I do not do any milking, because I am still too slow. Breakfast is at 7, then it's back in the barn, mucking out. My job is mostly driving the manure away. I have already earned being called "Mister". Afterwards, I go harvest the beets. I had not worked in the beets the last few days because it was too cold and snowy, but there are still 4 trucks to be loaded. We will probably be back tomorrow. Yes, there are a lot of cattle here. 6 horses, 17 calves, 4 dairy cows, 3 bulls, all in the stable. 30 were always in the bush until recently. Now that snow has fallen, they've also come into the stable. But these are steers, fed with straw and mucked out twice a week. Then there are 20 pigs. But Ella, I am far from being the foreman. That is Mr. Esau, a Mennonite. The farm belongs to an Englishman who lives in Winnipeg and only comes out occasionally. Besides me, there are 2 boys. One will stay over winter. I won't. As soon as my 4 weeks are up, I'll go back to Siemens, until I've found another job. I'm supposed to get $50, good for a start, but the work is hard for me, because I'm not used to the job. Don't know if Esau is always happy with me, but I'm doing my best. Well, it doesn't take forever, at least. I think, after the next harvest, I'm going to look for a job in Winnipeg. Because of the contract, I would like to endure. You signed your name on the contract, and when you complete it nobody can say anything

---

99   The Viscount Alexander of Tunis was the Governor-General of Canada.

about it later. What's more, I will have no travel debt. I got the bill today: $40.89. It's not a lot. I can pay it.

Dear Ella, if you would like to take part in the school party for new Canadians, just go. I will not be angry. In Winnipeg, there is also dancing when there's a wedding, but they don't have the right music. I'm afraid I have to start over with my dancing. Didn't see much of Winnipeg, either, but I don't think it's a very pretty city. Once you are here, we'll take a closer look at the city. Stay healthy and alert. Don't forget me, and come as soon as you are done there.

Your Hans.

P.S. I'll have been in Canada for 4 weeks soon, but I feel like I've been here a long time. Time is flying by.

23.11.49
Headingley

My dearest Ella!

Received your lovely letter as a treat after work this evening. Many thanks for that! I would like to receive one often, just to hear from you. I don't have a lot of interaction here. If I don't say anything, my boss won't say anything all day. I'm not very talkative myself, but this is a little too little. What's more, I work alone most of the time. With whom should I speak, with my horses? Well, they understand only English. Yes, my time will be up here soon—another week. I'm happy about that, as I liked it better at Siemens's. Last week, we loaded another 2 days of beets. They were all frozen and covered with snow, so we had to break them loose with a pick. Then, we were finally done. If I had stayed here, I would not have counted the days. But the crap I had to drive away, some days, like today, four sledges' full, one in the morning, then one from the pig stable, and two from the ox stall. Yesterday and today, they sold 20 cattle—thank God: less crap. Yesterday and today, it was particularly difficult, because the boss drove the cattle to Winnipeg, and I had to do almost everything here by myself. Milking yesterday, in the morning, too, which I can do if necessary—though not very fast. We could buy a cow, though, as I have learned something during this time.

When I am finished here, I want to go to Winnipeg for a few days, to visit all the people I know. Would like to see and talk to your parents, curious if they regret their decision. I would also prefer to go to Winnipeg, if the farmer would let go of me and the work opportunities were better. You can take the bus here but on Sunday, there is no bus from Headingley—only one returning from Winnipeg. But that can be done, if not, by hick-hiking, as it is called in English. If you come, I will go there, on foot if necessary. I often dream of my loved ones. I would like to write to my neighbours at home. Maybe there will be a message. I only fear troubling them. Maybe I'll hear some news soon. Enough for today! Now it's off to bed. Tomorrow is another day.

Goodnight, my little girl,

Your Hans.

26.11.49
Ottawa

My dearest Hans!

When I came home from school last night, your dear letter was waiting for me. First of all, of course I read it. It's a shame you can't read your mail right away. It is too long for me, even until the lunch break, so I read your letters right away, when I get it, even if my employer is next to me. On Thursday, Mom wrote me from Winnipeg. If you want to visit them, here is the address: 685 Logan Avenue. Until now, Papa has had no work, but I firmly believe he will find some after Christmas. You know, I don't want to stay until February 8th, but January 15th, or January 28th at the latest. I will go to the job centre on Friday. I so look forward to seeing you again—you can't imagine!

A newspaper for new Canadians is supposed to appear monthly and our teacher asked us, as an advance class, for our opinion and what we would like to find in it to read. We would like to read about anti-communism, about the country and people in Canada, job opportunities and so on. Hopefully, it will be distributed across Canada. So you have to pay $40 for your travel costs. My parents will probably have to pay $120. But that's not too much, and the main thing is that you are now in Canada. No matter how difficult and *unfamiliar the beginning, this time will pass. My time in Ottawa passed quickly, though in Russell, very slowly. Going to evening school has been a nice change, and I look forward to these hours. Well when I come, we'll speak English. Will anything come of that?! If we take it seriously, it has to work.*

See you soon!

Your Ella.

1.12.49
Ottawa

My dear Hans!

Received your dear letter today. I would also be happy if you could go to Winnipeg. But if it doesn't work, you can't do anything. At least we won't be as far apart as before. Tomorrow, I'm going to the job centre; I'm curious what the lady will say. Our school will soon be on vacation, too, which is really a shame. Imagine: I came home frozen last Sunday and Monday morning my old lady brought me her old fur coat! It is a bit short and old, but still warm and will do as a 3/4 length coat. Anyway, it will still serve me well. I'm very happy with it. I will wear my boots with it. Your beautiful handbag will accompany me on special occasions. It's pretty cold here. Wonder how I haven't slipped yet! On Tuesday, when I went to school, the snow was perfect for a snowball fight, only you were missing. Well, we'll make up for that, won't we?

My employer is sorry that I'm leaving. I found a piece of paper: "Girl for homework wanted." For the past few days, she has been moody, but it can't shake my resolve. I tell myself: only 6-8 weeks more. Regarding your loved ones: it would be good to write to the neighbours, though it might create problems for them. Would it be safer for them if the letter came from the Russian zone of Germany? Stay safe and sound.

Goodnight, my dearest!

Your Ella.

6.12.49
Headingley

My dearest Ella!

Last night, I received your precious letter before bed. Had a nice evening and, afterward, I lay awake and dreamed of my Ella. I often do that when I'm in my chamber after work. And, at night, I dream of my loved ones. So I'm not alone. Got a letter from my aunt yesterday.

Saturday, I went to Winnipeg to see your loved ones. When I arrived, only the children were home, and they fell right around my neck. Your dad was at work—he finally found some, and has to work on Sunday. Your Mom was at the train station to welcome acquaintances. The train arrived on Saturday at 8 a.m. Unfortunately, I did not know the time, or I would have gone there also. There were many young acquaintances. I slept at your parents.' They just have a small room for themselves, but they can also use the other rooms. I don't like the accommodations very much, but it is difficult to find accommodations with children. Now, for the time being, they have been accommodated and it will be fine. Hardi now speaks a lot more and only about Uncle Hein and his 2 tractors and horses. He is very enthusiastic about the farm. As he heard I also ride a horse, he wanted to drive manure with me. He looks very good. It was high time for the children to get out of the camp. If your dad could speak English, he could get good work in his trade. I listen to the radio to learn, and understand a lot of things on it, though, unfortunately, not everything. But that comes with time.

Yes, my time here is now over. I got my cheque today, the first $50 I have earned in Canada. The day after tomorrow, I'm free here. It's really a shame I can't stay here for the winter, because it's not a bad place. What makes things difficult for me is my foot. At first, it was pretty good, but now I'm sometimes so tired I could fall over, even if we don't do a lot. I have cramps more often, which is not very pleasant. But I want to endure as long as possible. Now, I'll see how it is with Siemens. It's the stupid thing with the contract. So many do not keep their contracts, even the newcomers coming over now. There will certainly be a commotion with the emigration again. I don't want to go and say that the work is too difficult for me. First of all, I wouldn't be believed, *and then, it would be bad for those who still want to come over here. Then, the Commission would act more strictly again. Don't think I will stay until October next year, though, because then it will be the same story with finding work. Will see what Siemens tells me.*

It won't be a problem for you to find work in Winnipeg. That's why you can come calmly. Beyond that, though, we want to welcome you in Manitoba. You no longer have to be afraid of the cold—that's really nice of your employer's mother. I am afraid, however, you have already become a grandmother. That would be fatal. What could I do with such an old woman? Just send me a picture or two, so I can really know whether or not this is true.

With writing from the Russian Zone, I think it would be better to have someone there, among the Russians, so that I could write like I did the first time. But that would also be better because East Germany will soon be Russian, too, unfortunately! I firmly hope to get messages from my loved ones soon. It would be a pleasure if someone were still alive and possibly in Germany. My sister is now 18 years old, nearly as grown as you. I think you would also get along well. Don't worry about me. It will be ok. I have to keep my will. It will work with God's help.

See you again!

Your Hans.

10.12.49
Ottawa

My dear Hans!

Already received your dear letter on Thursday, for which I give you my best thanks. Yes, it is already quite cold here. I already had mail from Mom. My siblings seem to have gotten very used to you and are so happy. But how much nicer will it be when your own children will fly to your neck? Mutti wrote that you wanted to come back today and stay for a few days. You have already spoken to Mr. Siemens? I am curious how he will answer you. I think if you would explain to him that you often have cramps, he should have a heart, and release you. *And you've grown so slim! Suddenly, I don't recognize you! Farm work is hard work, and your foot makes it even more difficult. I have often wondered how you were doing and feared it would be causing you difficulties. I know well, you have a strong will that accomplishes a lot, but I ask you, if it does not work, then introduce the matter to Mr. Siemens and you will get some guidance. I am glad that Dad found work, because he can hardly be without, and he has a family. I have already taken steps to get a travel discount for my parents and gave H. Borne's address. I'm curious if it will work.*

I have a good friend in the Russian Zone who would certainly be happy to send a letter on. Do not know if her father knows any Russians, but it is possible, because he is a tailor. So I make the suggestion, write the letter and send it here, and I will send it to Leipzig, and then we'll see how it goes. Just don't write anything that could harm the girl—you know how it is. Write as soon as possible. It would be wonderful if you got a message! When you wrote the first time, did you get an answer? Thank you very much for the words about the 23rd Psalm, because I can happily join in, "The Lord is my shepherd, I will not want." In English, we have a very good teacher and what we are working through is Grade 12, the last year before university. Hope that I can keep up my studies in Winnipeg, because I am always willing to learn. And you are, probably, too, right? I very much hope that we will be happy. I wish it from the bottom of my heart. Now my dear, brave Hans, take care of your health.

Your Ella.

17.12.49
Winnipeg

My dear Ella!

I had received your dear letter some time ago, but only had time to answer today. I came to Winnipeg a week later than I had planned. I didn't get off work from Siemens's right away, and only came here yesterday. I had wanted also to first speak to Mr. Siemens about whether I could take the time off. He could let me go now, and now it's time to look for work so that I could stay here. *The timing is pretty bad, but I hope to find something after the holidays. Before Christmas, there will be nothing, but hopefully things will improve later. I will probably go back to Siemens's later, Tuesday, and stay there over the holidays, if they're around. So this Christmas will not be as wonderful as the last one, but I am looking forward to your coming soon. Soon you will be here! If I find something here during this time, we will see each other more often. If you write me, though, send it to Siemens's, still.*

It is very cold here; it was down to minus 30, but you don't feel the cold very much, because it is a dry cold. You will feel it more in Ontario. But don't be afraid, because it will be fine. It went very well for me at Siemens's. I have recovered, and my foot has stopped hurting. It annoys me that I wrote about it to you.

I want to send you the letter to my neighbours, later. Maybe it will work. It would be good if the girl could pass it over to a Russian, but that is risky. I don't want her to have any trouble because of me. Maybe you can ask if it's possible, but write carefully, because everything goes through the censor over there!

You are probably counting the days until you can come. Just write me early enough so that we can pick you up from the train station. I already know Winnipeg somewhat, especially in this corner where your parents—and most of my acquaintances—live. Now, I want to close for today. Excuse my short letter. I'll write you a longer one over Christmas. Stay well, and come soon, as soon as possible! I wish you a Merry Christmas!

Kisses,

Your Hans.

P.S. See you in Winnipeg!!!!!!!!!!! Hope to celebrate together next Christmas.

Undated

My dear Hans!

For this year's Christmas celebrations, I wish you all the best and God's richest blessings. May these little gifts give you a little pleasure, despite your being alone. Unfortunately, we cannot be together to celebrate Christmas. On these days, we can think of last year and hope that God wants many more for us in the future. The gifts are pretty practical; hopefully, they will fit. The gloves are too thin for Manitoba but, since your coat is, too, you will be able to wear them together. And about my picture: I had the intention to send it to you for Christmas and it was meant to be a surprise. And so I needed many excuses (which you may have seen through!) to put it off for so long. Hopefully you think it looks like Ella; it was done on October 21st in anticipation of your coming. My wish is dear God will keep and protect you until we meet again and be with you at all times! Merry Christmas and happy New Year!

Your Ella.

20.12.49
Winnipeg

My dear Ella!

Though I sent a letter only a few days ago, I would still like to write to you. I want to go back to Siemens's today. I am now in the apartment of a friend, Edi Penner, who was our neighbour at home. I've slept here while I've been here. My last letter was written in a hurry, and with your relatives, the children around me. You know how it goes with the writing, then.

I have met a lot of acquaintances lately and listened around to how things are in terms of employment. It is now quite difficult to get something, but I hope to find something in the new year, when I'll come in, get a room and start looking. So many different thoughts and feelings go through your head in this time before Christmas. Above all, I am unsatisfied with Santa this year, but I hope the time will come again, when I can also place orders with him. There's

been a lot of activity in Winnipeg these days. I also went to the large depart-
ment stores, Eaton's and Hudson's Bay Co.

I continue to write from Siemens's, now. I arrived here at 1 p.m. and went
straight to the barn, which had not yet been cleaned out. I wanted to visit
Willy Hoch this morning, but he and his wife were both at work. They live
close to where I slept. I went into the house and met the Kasper and Ewy
family, all refugees. There is still a room available there, but it's a bit too big for
me; I would rather have a small one, just for myself, not be too far from Logan
Ave. Half of Backnang and Gronau are gathered in Winnipeg.

I came home and saw that Santa Claus had been here and left me a present.
It's a hard temptation for me, but I only have to endure 4 more days. What
did he bring me? How are you going to spend the holidays? Do you get them
free, or do you have to do even more these days?! Soon, you will have it behind
you. It has gotten a little cold, now 20 degrees below zero, or minus 25 degrees
Celsius. Uncle Siemens has just placed a big block of wood on for the night.
Tomorrow morning, the cold will be hard on the ears. We will probably go to
get hay, tomorrow, so that the holidays are quiet. I will soon have this chapter
behind me and a new one will begin. I wish you a Merry Christmas and hope
to be together again soon, with my Ella.

Many, many kisses,

Your Hans.

P.S. Please write me when you intend to come, so that I can cross out the days
in the calendar.

Christmas 1949
Ottawa

My dear Hans!

Your dear letter from December 20th arrived to my joy. There was a lot of
mail before Christmas. By Irma Ewy, Edith, Juliete, Tanta Otti, and Richard
and Lydia. As Edith writes, the "Leba" is dissolved, and every family has a
little room in Maubacher Höhe. Irma works for "Leder-Schwarz," Edith in a

153

stocking factory, and Nelly is on her way over the ocean, to the US. Everything is fine with Georg's lungs and, a few days ago, Schreyers received the guarantee from Butz! Kornel has met a widow with two children, so he will stay in Backnang. Hanni Schmidt and her mother stayed in St. Catherine's household. So, that's the most important news.

Now, I also want to write to you what Santa brought me. A leather-bound Bible, English, from the Martin family, a doily from Mutti, $5 from Mrs. Keefler's mother, $10 from Mr. and Mrs. Keefler, and 1 box of chocolates from their son and daughter. What did he bring you? Did Santa Claus from Ottawa bring you a little treat? Mom wrote that the Bornes asked them to look after the farm for a few days over Christmas.

On Christmas Eve we had snow and, after work, I opened Mom's and the Martins' packages, and read your dear letters. On the first day of Christmas, yesterday, I didn't finish until 4:00 p.m.; we had guests for Christmas lunch, a turkey! Then, I drove to the Martins' and, in the evening, went to church with Mrs. Martin. It was in the Metropolitan Tabernacle. There is a lot going on today, because tonight is the daughter's dance and at "lunch" we had a buffet for 10 people. I was surprised when everyone helped with clearing the table, and then, when I washed the dishes, the daughter and son dried! So I was done by 3 o'clock. It's been raining all day outside. According to the newspaper, you have snow and frost in Manitoba, real Christmas weather.

I'll be through this part of my life soon. Only 3 or 5 weeks left. I haven't given notice, yet, of the exact date. Incredible, eh? It seems unbelievable to me that I will be with my dear parents soon, soon, and often with you. All this time having been so alone, it will be very unusual for me to be with you all. Now, I wish you a happy New Year!

With many kisses,

Your Ella.

P.S. Do you remember New Year's Eve 1948? Do you miss it?!? This will not be as nice by a long shot.

25.12.49
Headingley

My dearest Ella!

I had already given up waiting for mail from you, only because I replied so late. How great my joy was when I received your lovely letter on the 24th. My sincere thanks for the beautiful picture and the lovely gifts, I jumped for joy when I saw your picture. I couldn't stand it until I was allowed to open it. I lifted it every day and guessed what could be in there. When you come, you'll get an extra-long kiss for it. For the time being, I do it in my mind.

Yesterday, the day passed very quickly. We got up late, so it took longer than usual to finish the stable. Siemens's married children came here and there was much joy. In the evening, we took care of the cattle and then quickly went on to the church in Pigeon Lake, as the community is called. A program was given by the Sunday school. When we came home, it was already 9 o'clock. I got out of the car to go and open the parcels right away. On the way, Mr. Siemens pressed one more gift into my hand. The gloves fit, but the shirt is a little big in the collar. The people here were also very curious about what I would get from you. Everyone loves your lovely picture. You could not have given me any greater joy; many thanks again! It is wonderful!

Yesterday, it started to storm in the morning, and, in the evening, it was very windy and cold. But today, it was nice. I went to church again, Mr. Siemens drove to Winnipeg with the whole family. I spent the afternoon asleep, took care of the cattle in the evening, and now, am writing a letter to my dear Ella. I don't know what I'm going to do tomorrow. I don't want to go to Winnipeg again, but if you were there, that would change things. But by the time you come, I'll already be there, and will have a room and perhaps work. Yes, I have many acquaintances there, from home and from Germany. Mrs. Berg is probably the oldest woman from Halbstadt, 91 years old.[100] She was also in Backnang.

....

100   Illustrations of the Mennonite Midwife Helene Berg, https://trailsofthepast.com/helene-berg/, accessed December 7, 2020.

Unfortunately, I could not finish my letter yesterday, so I'm continuing to write this on the 26th, today. I didn't enjoy last night; my hosts came back late. In the meantime, there was a visitor so I could no longer write. So I'll keep at it today. The kids went out for the evening. I was invited to go, too, but didn't feel like it. I thought, maybe, I should be joyous here, even if it is forced, as my parents might not have enough to eat in Siberia today. If my parents are still alive, they will have thought of me these days.

You write that you want to stop on February 28th. I think you meant January, right? Or do you want to stay there for so long? Why are you afraid of quitting? Do you think your employers will be mean to you then? They knew you weren't going to stay anyway. Mr. Siemens is very nice, but I think he would prefer that I don't find a job, so I will stay here. It is very difficult, now, because many workers are now being laid off after the holidays, and work can only be found through connections. I want to hope for good luck. This worries me because, without work, I cannot last long. After all, I want to earn something. It's been 8 weeks now that I've been in Canada. When all else fails, we can travel back to Gronau, can't we? Or do you not feel like it? Are you happy that you can leave Ottawa soon? I'm terribly happy. These weeks seem longer to me than the months in Germany. Will we still understand each other? Or have we grown far apart? I hope not.

28.12.49
Winnipeg

Dearest Ella!

I had the opportunity to drive to Winnipeg with Siemens's car yesterday, so I took advantage of it. I'm going back today. Yesterday was the silver wedding at Rupp's[101], and it was getting late when we left, so I went to Paul Barchet's, who wasn't home, to sleep. Since it is still a little early to go to your relatives', I want to finish my letter to mine. Your dad was invited to a wedding yesterday. They had the ceremony in the house, because it would have cost $25 in the church, and they couldn't afford it. Viktor only started working a few

---

101   Rudolph Rupp was a relative of Ella's stepfather, Johann Jacob Rupp.

weeks ago. That's how it is with the refugees. It's not that bad; they will get ahead later.

There was a lot of hellos just now, as the children were all home. I had a duvet of your parents in my crate; when I brought it out, your siblings flew to my neck like a couple of wild ones! Hardi now speaks a lot. He is very interested in machines. When we went to Rupp's yesterday, he saw a car with a lifting crane on the way, and wanted to stop and see it would do. He talks a lot, and always about Uncle Hein's tractor; he says he will get one, the green one (it's bigger)!

Yesterday, I saw a photograph of you from the year 1940. In it, you look very much like my little sister. I dreamt of my relatives again last night. In my dream, someone wanted to tell me where my relatives went but I wasn't given the address. Will I ever find them?

Christmas is nice when you can spend it with your loved ones. Last year, it was nicer. Do you remember? But this year, you also pleased me greatly with your lovely picture. When you come here, we will undo the past year, except for what we have learned from it, and will continue where we left off when you left. It was a long, long year, and we only saw each other for 2 days the whole time. But we have not forgotten each other. Do you still love me? Just write it to me so I have it in black and white. And when you come, I want to hear it.

For today, I wish you all the best. Good luck to us both in the New Year and see you again soon. Stay healthy and true to your Hans!

Many kisses,

Your impatient Hans.

P.S. Write me a long letter very soon, so that the final few days before you come don't feel too long.

30.12.49
Ottawa

My dearest!

Thank you so much for your lovely Christmas presents; I really like the scarf! Wore it for the first time yesterday. You know, I needed something just like it and thought about buying a scarf. So you bought me something very appropriate.

Now, the latest, dear Hans: I gave my notice today! Hopefully, I will be with you on January 20th! I can hardly believe it! I can't be quite sure, yet, because my employer can insist I stay until the 28th. But hope for the best. When I told her, she was surprised, but now everything is as usual. My employer's mother has just praised me just as she always does, saying my kitchen will be very clean. The long letter won't be coming, because I'd rather say everything orally than write. Don't be upset with me. I can't sit down long enough to write. I just think, I'll be travelling soon. I was happy to hear you were back in Winnipeg. I am particularly pleased that you like my picture.

Today is December 30th, when you asked my parents for permission to marry you. Remember when we sat there waiting for the right opportunity? Engaged for 1 year tomorrow and almost never been together since. But we'll see each other again soon! I don't just think I love you, I know I love you very, very dearly! It was really a long, long year. But this separation will soon be over. Hooray!!

Now, I wish you much success in looking for a job, though I would prefer if you didn't have one when I come—otherwise, you won't be able to meet me at the train station! Am I very selfish? You're coming anyway, right?!

With many kisses,

Your Ella.

See you soon! I won't be unfaithful!

3.1.50
Pigeon Lake

My dearest Ella!

I received your dear Christmas parcel several days ago, but I hesitated to answer, so that the letters would not cross. If there is mail from you, I sense it. At half past eleven, I went to the mailbox, which is on the highway, about 200m from the farmyard. If something is inside, it is turned perpendicular, so you can see from the yard whether the mail has been delivered. Now, by this time, it had usually come, so I went to see if the box had been turned and, when I stood in front of it, it was empty. I turned around, somewhat annoyed about my sleepy head, and with the wind behind me, went back. At the yard, I turned again to look back at the mailbox and saw the mail truck stopping at the neighbours. So, back again to the mailbox I went and, this time, there were 2 letters, your dear one and one from Hugo. So, I didn't run twice for nothing. We had a snowstorm yesterday, and today it's 23 degrees below zero, with a wind from the northwest that pretty much cuts our noses.

I am glad the scarf pleases you. It is good if you can ask a mother-in-law and she can give advice. I would have loved to have bought you something else. If I had stayed at Esau's, I might have been able to. Well, let's hope that better times will come.

I'm glad you have given your notice, but I don't think your employer will be so petty. Sooner or later, you will go away. After all, your immigration contract is ultimately none of her business. I would like to pick you up, but it would be better if I had work by then and had thus gained a foothold in Winnipeg. So it will depend on whether I'm working or not. At the end of this week or next, I will definitely go in and look for a room. I can still keep afloat for several weeks. So I expect this to be my last letter from Siemens's. If you answer me right away, I will still get your message; if not, write your parents, and I can find out when you'll arrive.

These days were also full of memories for me: Christmas, Thomashof, Ludwigsburg, Backnang, and last December 30th and 31st. This past year started very seriously. But soon, it will be nice. This time, my sun will rise in the southeast and come to Manitoba. Maybe it will be warmer here, though whether the snow will melt by then is questionable. But it will feel much warmer. At least my Spring is coming this January. I sit here by the Stove, one side warm, the other, toward the window, cold. There is no proper heating here. Tomorrow, it should be 30 below zero. Hopefully, my sun will come soon. Otherwise, it will still be cold in Manitoba!

For today, many warm regards from your John and kisses, many times, from your Hans.

13.

A new life

The Rupps had moved to Winnipeg after a short stay of only about six weeks in Springstein, Manitoba. The harvest at the Borne farm had essentially been completed already by the time they arrived. The church offered them an empty house beside the church, but Johann Jacob had had enough of living in camps or with the help of others. Sophie Rupp was walking with them on Logan Avenue one day, when she spotted a Ukrainian woman and asked if she would take the Rupp family in. The daughter gave up her bed to Amalie, Johann Jacob, and Hardy, while she and Lydia slept on a davenport together by the stove, in the middle of the house. Amalie would do the washing for everyone in the kitchen and kept the house warm.

Johann found a room at 859 Bannatyne Avenue, in Winnipeg. He found employment at Canadian Sportswear, a company of Silpit Industries, as a cutter, earning twenty-five cents an hour. Ella came to Winnipeg after completing her one year of immigration service as a domestic servant in Ottawa. She found work sewing in a garment factory and earned up to a dollar an hour on piecework. When Ella arrived from Ottawa, she was allowed to sleep on

Johann working as a cutter 1950.

the sofa in the living room with the Rupps. In March of 1950, the Rupps rented a room and kitchen in an old house on Manitoba Avenue. They rented another small room upstairs, but the landlord would not allow Johann to move in with them. So Ella and Johann found two rooms and a kitchen on the third floor at 518 Bannatyne Avenue in which to start their married life.

Johann and Ella were married on June 10, 1950, in the basement of First Mennonite Church at Alverstone Street and Notre Dame Avenue, which was under construction at the time. They became active members at First Mennonite and remained so for the rest of their lives.

Ella Weber/Johann Franz wedding 1950.

Ella and Johann at Christmas 1950.

*Ella and Johann on
Garfield St. in 1951.*

The Franzes, the Rupps, and Johann Rupp's nephew Erwin Andres with his wife Erna, bought a house together in 1951 at 1103 Garfield Street in Winnipeg's West End. The three families shared the house until the Andreses moved, in 1952, to St. Catherines, Ontario where Erwin's mother, Tante Otti (Opa Rupp's sister), then lived. Erwin got a job with General Motors in the manufacturing plant there, and they raised three children together: Linda, Irene, and Rudy. The Rupps then took the main floor and the Franzes the upper, all sharing one bathroom. In July of 1956, the Rupps bought a house at 986 Dominion Street, a couple of blocks away from the Franzes'. Johann Rupp had found work at John Wood, a boiler manufacturer. When Lydia and Hardy were older, Amalie took up part-time work cleaning houses.

Hardy & Lydia (back row), baby Ingrid (centre), Willie & Marg (front row) Christmas 1957.

Marg, Willie, Ingrid and Ella (L to R), camping 1959.

Ingrid, Willie, baby Monika, and Marg (L to R) 1963.

Johann bought his first car in 1954, a Volkswagen Beetle and a Klepper fold-boat soon after. Camping, fishing and car trips across Canada were favourite outings of his, when the time was available.

In 1956, Johann discovered the address of his mother Elisabet and his sister Margaret (Gretel) through the International Red Cross. They had been deported to Siberia in 1946 and were living in Novosibirsk. A letter of his from the early half of 1950 had been forwarded to his mother a year later, but he did not receive the letter that she sent in reply. Starting in 1956, Johann and his mother then wrote to each other monthly until her death in 1975. In her letters to my father, my grandmother writes that Johann's father David must be dead as he would have otherwise found them already.

Lydia Rupp married a Peter Dyck (not the same as MCC's Peter Dyck) and they moved to Rexdale in Toronto and then to Mississauga, Ontario where they raised two children Monica and Oliver. Hardy Rupp also moved to Mississauga where he married Gwen Allen and raised a son Jason.

In 1979, Johann and Ella bought a cottage at Pinawa Bay near Lac du Bonnet, which remains in the family. Ella still had the desire to travel to foreign destinations, so together they travelled to Hawaii, New Zealand and Australia, as well as back to Germany several times.

Johann worked at Canadian Sportswear for 40 years, retiring in 1990 at the age of sixty-five. He became a marker, laying out the patterns for the cutters who cut the cloth to manufacture outer wear. Ella and John raised four children, Margaret, me, Bill, Ingrid and Monika. In later years, Ella went to work as a salesclerk at Eaton's Downstairs, an outlet store at Polo Park. She maintained an interest in business, practiced her typing, and studied French at St. Boniface College.

Johann's sister Margaret, alongside her husband Adam Mündt, was able to emigrate to Germany in 1992 with two of their three daughters, one son-in-law, and a granddaughter. Johann and Ella visited them twice: once in 1993 and again in 2001. It had been more than fifty years since Johann and Margaret had seen each other.

Johann Rupp had passed away in 1978, while Amalie Rupp lived independently at Autumn House (except for her last 4 months at the Deer Lodge Centre) until she passed away at the age of 97 in 2005.

Ella passed away from cancer in 2003 and Johann followed her in 2004, also succumbing to cancer. It was a hard blow for Johann to lose Ella after some fifty years together. He reread all of the letters that he and Ella had exchanged in the year they were apart. It was also hard, for my sisters and I, to lose our mother, father and grandmother in a relatively short time period. We treasure our memories of them.

EPILOGUE

Ella and Johann continued to support the work of MCC in their lifetimes.[102] Here is an excerpt from MCC's vision and mission statement: "Mennonite Central Committee (MCC), a worldwide ministry of Anabaptist churches, shares God's love and compassion for all in the name of Christ by responding to basic human needs and working for peace and justice. MCC envisions communities worldwide in right relationship with God, one another and creation." When the Vietnamese "boat people" came to Canada in the late 1970s, Ella and Johann contributed to the cause.[103] The plight of refugees continues to occupy a soft spot in my heart to this day.

I was exploring the possibility of travelling to Ukraine with my parents to see the old country when Ella became ill, and we spoke no more of it. But in the fall of 2018, my sisters and I, along with a couple of brothers-in-law, did travel to Ukraine to see what we could find. In Lviv, we found the corner store that our maternal grandparents had run, and the apartment building where they lived, as well as the church where Amalie married her second husband, Johann. We explored our ancestral village of Dornfeld and found Amalie's childhood home. We stopped at Mykolaiv (a place nearby to where Wilhelm and Amalie farmed the land) and also made a day trip to Poland, including to Krowica Sama, where Johann Rupp was born.

Then we flew to Kiev and joined TourMagination's tour of Ukraine which took us to the former villages of the Chortitza and Molotschna colonies. We were able to briefly see Hoffental, Andreburg, Halbstadt, Gnadenfeld, and Sparrau. From Odessa, I carried on to Russia with TourMagination to see St.

102   Mennonite Central Committee (Canada), https://mcccanada.ca, accessed December 5, 2020.

103   Wikipedia, s.v. "Vietnamese boat people," last modified on March 9, 2021, at 01:12 (UTC), https://en.wikipedia.org/wiki/Vietnamese_boat_people.

Petersburg and Moscow. I then flew on to Novosibirsk in Siberia to meet my first cousin Anna Achmetchanowa and her family for the first time and to visit my paternal grandmother's grave. I also saw the apartment building the family moved into in 1960 after living in wooden barracks for 14 years. The article "A Journey in Time" is available on the website of the Mennonite Historical Society of Alberta.[104]

Ella and Johann's descendants include four children, eight grandchildren, and at my time of writing this, eight great-grandchildren, all in Canada.

---

104   Franz, Bill, "A Journey in Time," *The MHSA Chronicle*, Volume XXII Number 1, March 2019, https://mennonitehistory.org/wp-content/uploads/Newsletter-No.-1-April-2019.pdf.

MAPS

1. Migration Chronology of an Old Flemish Congregation in Polish-Prussia. William Schroeder. http://www.mennonitechurch.ca/programs/archives/holdings/Schroeder_maps/028.pdf. Used by permission.

2. Brenkenhoffswalde Franztal and Neudessau. William Schroeder. http://www.mennonitechurch.ca/programs/archives/holdings/Schroeder_maps/029.pdf. Used by permission.

3. Migration from the Vistula to South Russia. William Schroeder in Huebert, Helmut T., Molotschna, Historical Atlas, 2. Winnipeg. Springfield Publishers, 2003. Used by permission.

4. The Moloschna River and adjacent Colonies (in 1806). Huebert, Helmut T., Molotschna Historical Atlas, 3. Winnipeg. Springfield Publishers, 2003. Used by permission.

5. Map of the German Colonies in the Molotschna in South Russia in 1836. Huebert, Helmut T., Molotschna Historical Atlas, 4. Winnipeg. Springfield Publishers, 2003. Used by permission.

6. The Molotschna Mennonite Colony according to Hippenmayer, in 1852. Huebert, Helmut T., Molotschna Historical Atlas, 6. Winnipeg. Springfield Publishers, 2003. Used by permission.

7. Molotschna Colony Region in 1998. Huebert, Helmut T., Molotschna Historical Atlas, 15. Winnipeg. Springfield Publishers, 2003. Used by permission.

8. Halbstadt and Neighbouring Villages in 1913. William Schroeder in Huebert, Helmut T., Molotschna Historical Atlas, 40. Winnipeg. Springfield Publishers, 2003. Used by permission

9. Plan von Dornfeld, Gezeichnet nach einem Plan von Bürgermeister Jakob Bechtloff (vom Winter 1914/15). Seefeldt, Fritz, H. Schweitzer, and J. Krämer, Pfälzer Wandern: Kolonisation, Umsiedlung, Vertriebung, Heimkehr. Dornfelds Chronik II. Eutin: Struve's Buchdruckerei und Verlag, 1959.

10. Map Ten - Lviv to Leipzig: Relocation of the Rupp Family 1940-1945. Trails of the Past, 2021.

11. Map Eleven - Leipzig to Cuxhaven: Relocation of the Rupp Family 1945-1949. Trails of the Past, 2021.

12. Map Twelve - Halbstadt (Molochans'k) to Hohensalza (Inowroclaw): Elisabet & Margaret Franz 1943-45. Trails of the Past, 2021.

13. Map Thirteen - Wehrmacht 1. Mountain Division: Molochans'k to Sofia 1941-43. Trails of the Past, 2021.

14. Map Fourteen - Wehrmacht 1. Mountain Division: Sofia to Linz 1943-45. Trails of the Past, 2021.

15. Map Fifteen - Linz to Cuxhaven: Johann Franz 1945-49. Trails of the Past, 2021.

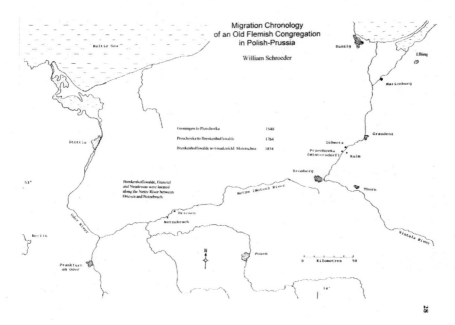

Migration Chronology from Groningen, the Netherlands to Prussia to South Russia.

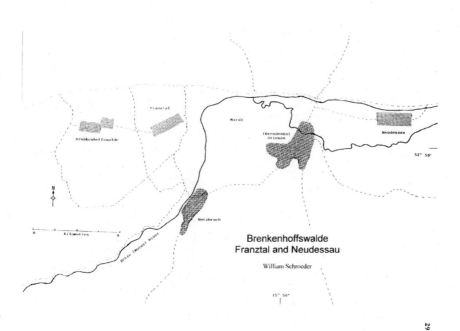

Brenkenhofswalde, Franztal, and Neudessau in Polish-Prussia.

171

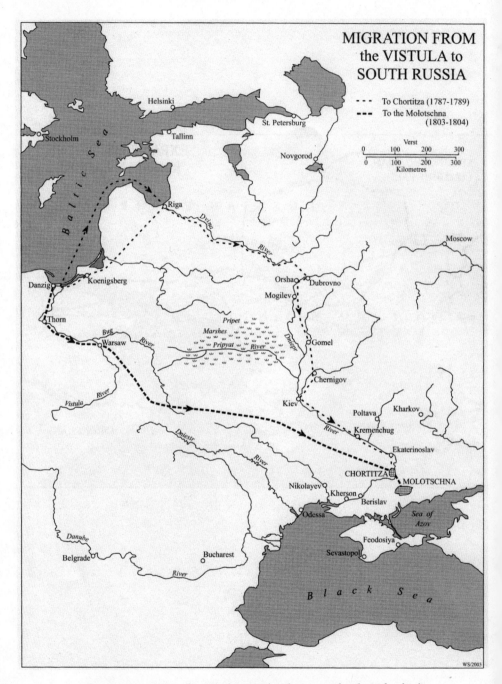

Migration from the Vistula to South Russia (to Chortitza and to the Molotschna).

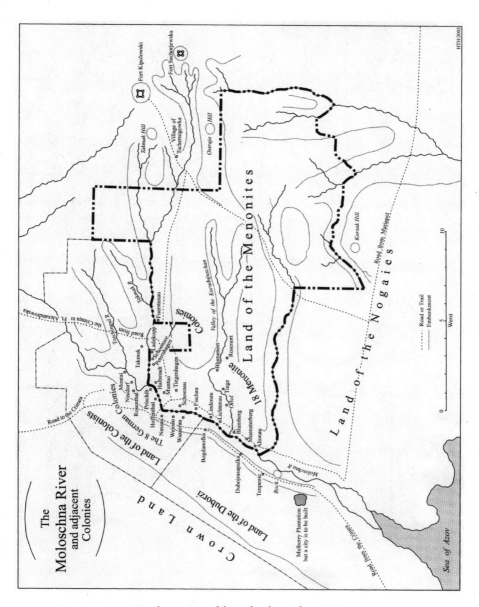

First known map of the Molotschna Colony 1806.

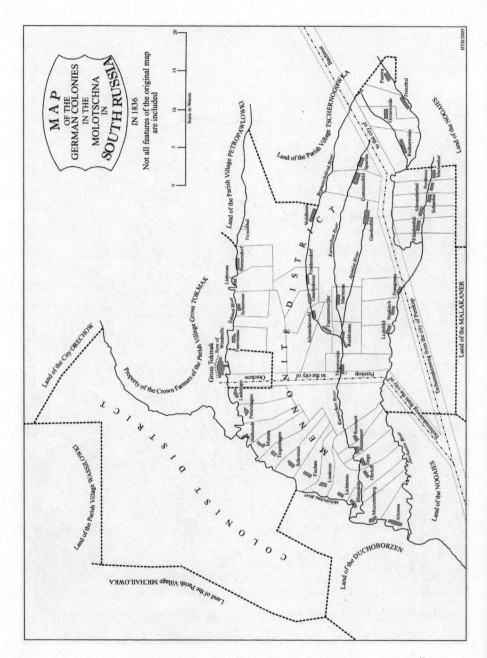

Map of the German Colonies in the Molotschna 1836.

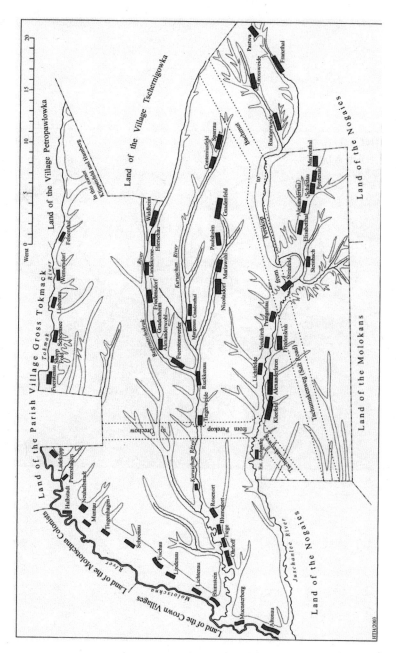

The Molotschna Mennonite Colony 1852.

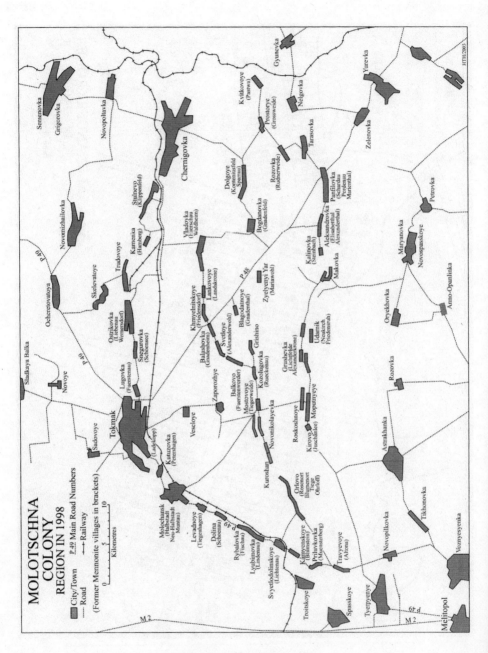

Molotschna Colony Region 1998.

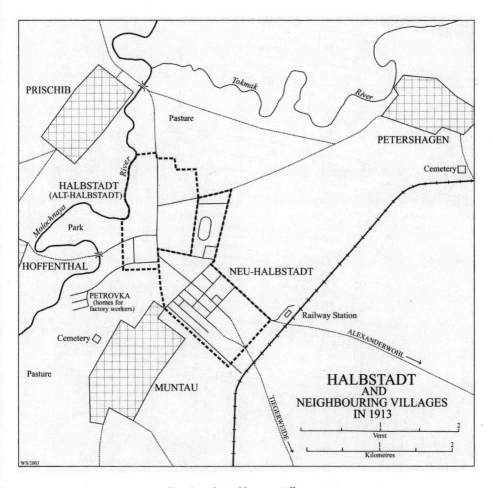

Halbstadt and Neighbouring Villages, 1913.

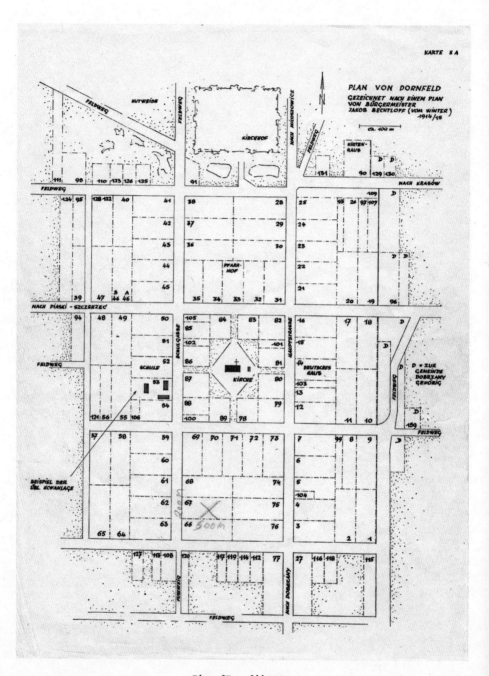

Plan of Dornfeld 1914.

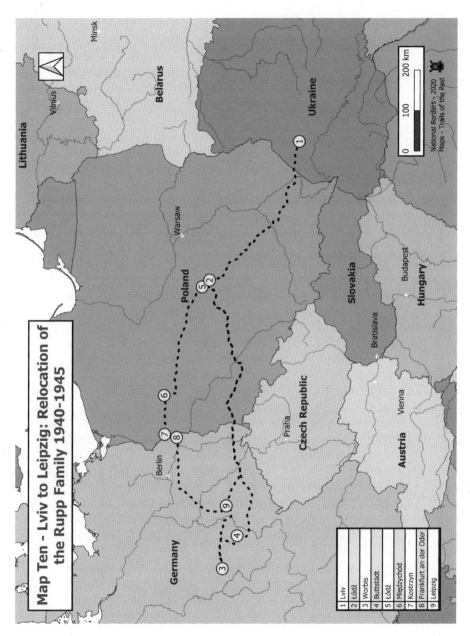

Lviv to Leipzig: Relocation of the Rupp family 1940-45.

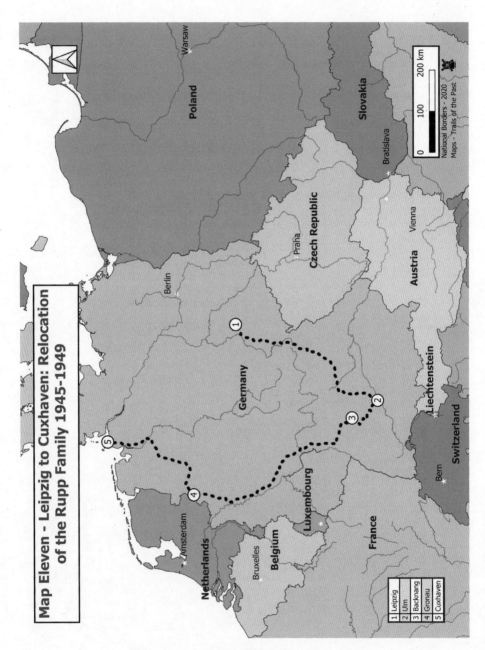

Leipzig to Cuxhaven: Relocation of the Rupp family 1945-49.

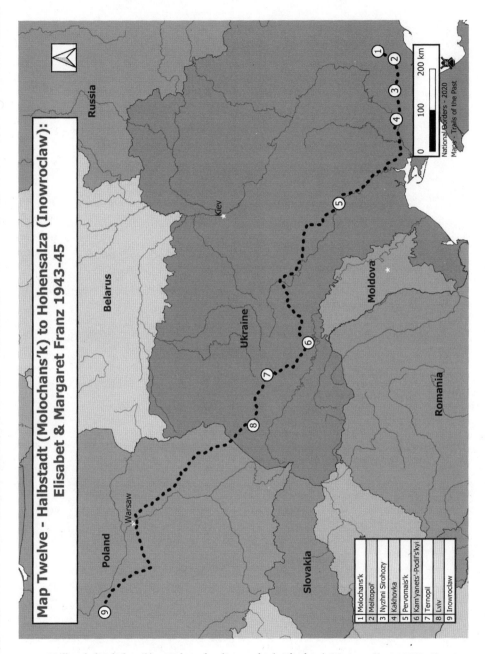

Halbstadt (Molochans'k) to Hohensalza (Inowroclaw): Elisabet & Margaret Franz 1943-45.

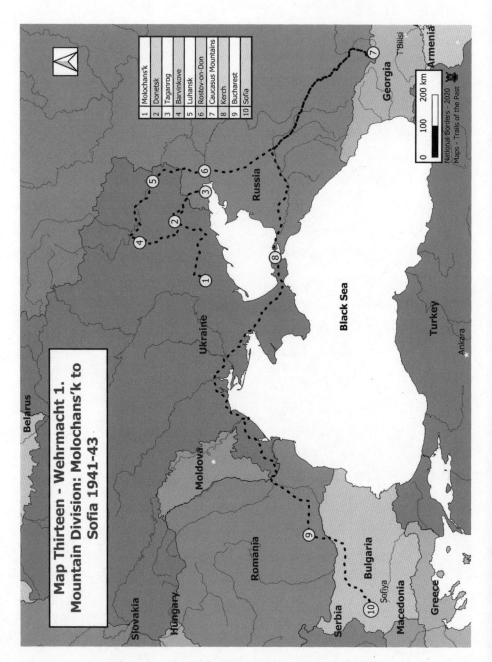

Wehrmacht 1. Mountain Division: Molochans'k to Sofia 1941-43.

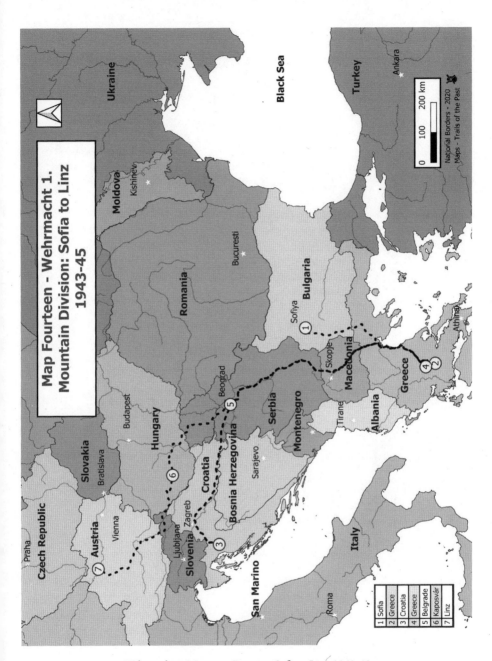

Wehrmacht 1. Mountain Division: Sofia to Linz 1943-45.

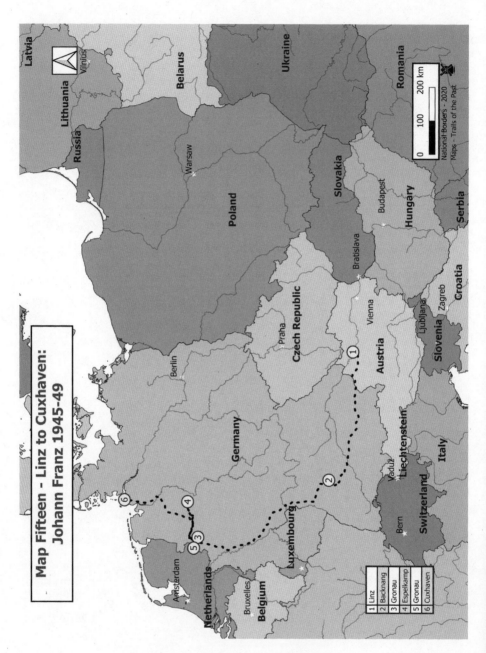

Linz to Cuxhaven: Johann Franz 1945-49.

FAMILY TREE

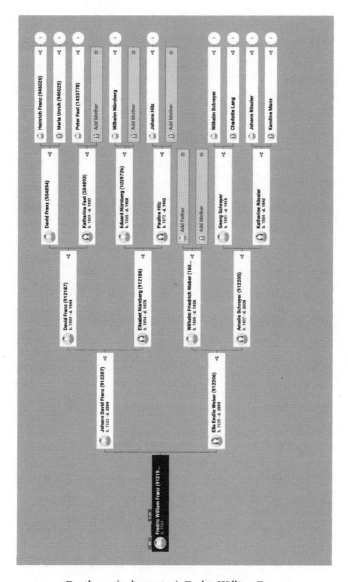

Family tree (pedigree view): Fredric William Franz.

APPENDIX

Deutsche Dienststelle

für die Benachrichtigung der nächsten Angehörigen
von Gefallenen der ehemaligen deutschen Wehrmacht

Deutsche Dienststelle (WASt), 13400 Berlin

LUFTPOST
Herrn
Fredric William Franz

Geschäftszeichen:
(Bei Rückfragen bitte Geschäftszeichen,
Namen und Geburtsdaten angeben)
II B 113 Franz, Johann
* 24.02.1925
Bearbeiter/in:
Herr Kuhn
Zimmer:

Telefon:
(0 30) 4 19 04 116
Telefax:
(0 30) 4 19 04 100
Datum:
01.12.2016

Sehr geehrter Herr Franz,

auf Ihr Schreiben vom 17.11.2015 teile ich Ihnen mit, dass die Personalpapiere (Wehr-
pass, Wehrstammbuch, Personalakte) Ihres Vaters hier nicht vorliegen; sie sind vermut-
lich durch Kriegseinwirkungen verloren gegangen. Aus diesem Grund ist ein lückenloser
Nachweis über die Dienstzeit nicht möglich.

Aus dem sonstigem Schriftgut der ehemaligen Wehrmacht wird Folgendes bestätigt:

F R A N Z, Johann, geboren am 24.02.1925 in Andreburg / Ukraine

Heimatanschrift: 1944   Mutter: Elisabeth Franz, Halbstadt / Ukraine,
                                      Goethestr. 5

Erkennungsmarke: -96-   F. Laz. Geb. Brig.
                                      (Feldlazarett Gebirgs-Brigade)

Truppenteile:
am   06.02.1944   Feldlazarett 54 (motorisiert)
                                      Unterstellung: 1. Gebirgs-Division
                                      *Einsatzraum: Kroatien *)*

ab   07.02.1944) 4. Kompanie Feld-Ersatz-Bataillon 654
und am   11.04.1944)

ab   11.04.1944) 2. Kompanie Feld-Ersatz-Bataillon 654
und am   20.09.1944) *Das Feld-Ersatz-Bataillon 654 unterstand der 104.
                                      Jäger-Division.
                                      Einsatzraum: Februar-September 1944 West-
                                      Griechenland *)*

Dienstgebäude: Fahrverbindungen: Sprechzeiten: Zahlungen bitte   Geldinstitut   Kontonummer   Bankleitzahl
Eichborndamm 179   Bus 221   Mo.-Mi. 9.00-14.00 Uhr bargeldlos an die   Postbank Berlin   56-100   100 100 10
13403 Berlin   U-Bhf. Rathaus   Do. 10.00-18.00 Uhr   Landeshauptkasse
E-Mail: St. ihlenburg@dd-wast.de Reinickendorf (U8) Fr. 9.00-13.00 Uhr 10789 Berlin Berliner Sparkasse 0 990 007 600   100 500 00
Internet: http://www.dd-wast.de

WASt 121 (8/05)

Deutsche Dienststelle military records of Johann Franz, page 1.

187

- 2 -

Weitere Truppenmeldungen liegen nicht vor. Ich weise darauf hin, dass das hier verwaltete Schriftgut der ehemaligen deutschen Wehrmacht und sonstiger militärischer und militärähnlicher Verbände unvollständig ist.

Kriegsgefangenschaft:
Aufzeichnungen über einen eventuellen Aufenthalt in Kriegsgefangenschaft konnten nicht festgestellt werden.

Ich hoffe Ihnen mit meinen Ausführungen geholfen zu haben.

Die Deutsche Dienststelle ist bemüht, Anfragen nicht nur zuverlässig, sondern auch schnellstmöglich zu beantworten. Bedingt durch die große Anzahl der Auskunfts-Ersuchen, die vielfach zudem wegen ihrer Komplexität einen besonders hohen Zeitaufwand erfordern, muss dennoch grundsätzlich mit einer Bearbeitungsdauer von mehreren Monaten gerechnet werden. Ich bedauere dies und hoffe, auf Grund der vorgenannten Erklärung, nachträglich auf Ihr Verständnis für die späte Beantwortung Ihrer Anfrage.

Mit freundlichen Grüßen

Im Auftrag

Kuhn

⁾ Vergleich: Tessin, Georg: Verbände und Truppen d. deutschen Wehrmacht u. Waffen-SS im Zweiten Weltkrieg 1939-45, Osnabrück, 1973 ff.

Deutsche Dienststelle military records of Johann Franz, page 2.

188